THE BEDTIME FAMILY devotional

90 DEVOTIONS TO HELP YOUR FAMILY LOVE AND LIVE FOR GOD

RUTH AND PATRICK SCHWENK

BETHANYHOUSE
a division of Baker Publishing Group
Minneapolis, Minnesota

Published by Bethany House Publishers
Minneapolis, Minnesota
BethanyHouse.com

Bethany House Publishers is a division of
Baker Publishing Group, Grand Rapids, Michigan

Printed in the United States of America

Library of Congress Cataloging-in-Publication Data
Names: Schwenk, Ruth | Schwenk, Patrick, author.
Title: The bedtime family devotional : 90 devotions to help your family love and live for God / Ruth Schwenk and Patrick Schwenk.
Description: Minneapolis, Minnesota : Bethany House Publishers, a division of Baker Publishing Group, [2024]
Identifiers: LCCN 2023037762 | ISBN 9780764242403 (paperback) | ISBN 9780764242854 (casebound) | ISBN 9781493445288 (ebook)
Subjects: LCSH: Parents --Prayers and devotions. | Parent and child —Religious aspects—Christianity. | Bedtime prayers.
Classification: LCC BV4845 .S34 2009 | DDC 242/.645—dc23/eng/20231012
LC record available at https://lccn.loc.gov/2023037762

The authors are represented by the Brock, Inc. Agency.

Baker Publishing Group publications use paper produced from sustainable forestry practices and post-consumer waste whenever possible.

24 25 26 27 28 29 30   7 6 5 4 3 2 1

THE
BEDTIME
FAMILY
devotional

Books by Ruth Schwenk

To Tyler, Bella, Noah, and Sophia:
You were made to love God and live for God.
May He bless you, protect you, and work through you for His purposes.
We love you, are proud of you, and believe in you.

Contents

Section One

What Do I Want My Child to KNOW?   15

Section Two

What Do I Want My Child to BE?   79

Section Three

What Do I Want My Child to DO?   145

Dear Parents,

God loves the family. He loves your family. And one of the greatest joys we have is, with God's help, the opportunity to pass on faith to the next generation!

One of the most sobering comments in the Bible about passing on faith is found in Judges 2:10. In speaking about the Israelites, it says, "After that whole generation had been gathered to their ancestors, another generation grew up who knew neither the Lord nor what he had done for Israel." One generation knew the Lord. They had seen His power, goodness, and faithfulness and were grounded in their faith. But in just one generation, a grounded generation gave birth to an ungrounded one.

As parents, we do not want to make the same mistake! This is why we are so excited to provide a resource like *The Bedtime Family Devotional*. It is both **helpful** and **hopeful**! It helps parents, but it also reminds each of us that by God's grace, we can with confidence raise kids and release kids to live for Jesus!

The Bedtime Family Devotional is a ninety-day devotional to help parents root their children in faith before releasing them into the world. Divided into three parts (thirty devotions each), we answer three questions:

- **What do we want our children to KNOW?** This first set of devotions is geared toward helping kids understand basic theology. For example, we'll cover questions such as *What is God like? Who is Jesus? What is grace?*

- **What do we want our children to BE?** The second set of devotions is designed to help cultivate virtue or character in the life of a child. Beyond knowing God with their heads, we want kids to grow up and truly be transformed into the image of Christ.

- **What do we want our children to DO?** And finally, the last set of devotions is meant to help turn families outward, looking at the kind of life Jesus calls each of us to. We'll talk about what it looks like to live a life of love for God and for others.

We've been in pastoral ministry for nearly twenty-five years. We've written numerous books and devotionals for moms, children, and families, and even a book on how to love your spouse with kids in the house. Passing on faith and helping others do the same is so important to us that we even created several online ministries.

BUT . . . we are really excited about *this* resource. We are confident God will use it in powerful ways to grow your family closer to one another and to Jesus!

We hope and pray that this book helps you love God more fully and live for Him more faithfully. We are in this with you! May it be said of our children that they were found righteous in their generation. We are praying for you and pressing on with you.

In Christ,
Ruth and Patrick Schwenk

How to Use This Devotional

The following is a brief description of what to expect and how to best use *The Bedtime Family Devotional*.

What should we expect?

- Each devotion should take five to ten minutes.
- Devotions are written for a child to read but also work great for a parent to read to their child.
- Each day has a **key verse**, **key idea**, **devotion** (300–350 words), **action step** that drives home the key idea, and a **family prayer**.
- We recommend doing each day's devotion just before bed. After a busy day, it is the perfect way to wind down and fill your child's head and heart with God's love and truth before going to sleep.
- Finally, have fun! There is no greater joy than loving and living for Jesus! So, with God's help, enjoy every moment of praying together. Talking. Teaching. And dreaming of all the things God wants to do in you and through your family!

What could our bedtime devotional time look like?

1. Begin by praying with and for your child. Ask God to prepare your hearts as a family to hear His voice and learn, asking that your child continue to grow into whom Jesus wants your child to be.
2. Have your child read the key verse at the top of the devotion.

3. Give your child a few minutes to read the devotion.

4. Take a minute to explain or answer any questions your child may have.

5. Allow your child a few minutes to complete the action step, offering any help if necessary.

6. And lastly, pray the family prayer together at the end of the devotion. This completes your bedtime family devotional time!

Section One

What Do I Want My Child to KNOW?

What are some of the most important things to know about God and the Bible? This section helps answer that question in thirty devotions! We'll make simple and practical the important truths every Christian should know.

The God Who Had No Beginning and Has No End

Key Verse

Before the mountains were born
or you brought forth the whole world,
from everlasting to everlasting you are God.

Psalm 90:2

Key Idea

God *has been* there for us, *is* there for us, and *will always be* there for us.

Do you remember the day you were born? Well, you probably don't remember that day, but you probably remember the *date*—your birthday! Every year, you likely gather with your family or friends and eat lots of good food and open presents. All of this for YOU—celebrating and giving thanks for when your life began!

You have really grown and changed since you were born. Your body has gotten bigger and stronger. You have learned new things and you are smarter! You can talk and share how you feel differently than you could when you were little. Every year since your life began, you have been getting older, bigger, and wiser—you are changing.

But God is different.

He did not start to exist when someone else made Him. There was never a time when God was not around. He didn't need a birthday! No one had to create God. He doesn't change or get bigger or wiser, stronger, or smarter. He has always been, always is, and always will be. God is eternal! The psalmist says in Psalm 90:2, "Before the mountains were born or you brought forth the whole world, from everlasting to everlasting you are God."

Because God is eternal, we can always count on Him. Whether we look backward at our life or look forward, God is always there. He never changes, and He will always be there for us. If that makes your brain hurt a little when you think about it, that's okay! Even for moms and dads, it's hard to wrap our minds around it. But this truth about God should also give us hope.

It should help us to feel safe when everything around us is changing. It should bring us joy because no matter what happens in our lives, God will be there!

Action Step

Take a minute and share with your family what you **feel** when you think about God as eternal.

Prayer

Father, thank You for the reminder that You are eternal—You always have been, You are, and You will always be. Help us to trust You and to remember that You are the God who never changes. Fill us with joy and hope. In Jesus' name, amen.

2

The God Who Can Do All

Key Verses:

In the beginning God created the heavens and the earth. Now the earth was formless and empty, darkness was over the surface of the deep, and the Spirit of God was hovering over the waters.
And God said, "Let there be light," and there was light.

Genesis 1:1–3

Key Idea

God is so powerful that nothing is impossible for Him.

Have you ever walked along a beach, with the sand squishing through your toes and felt really small compared with how BIG the ocean is?

All of creation—the trees, the oceans, birds, mountains, flowers, and a whole lot more—point to a Creator. Like a great Artist, God created all that there is. But this Artist, this Creator, didn't use paintbrushes, pens, or pencils. He didn't use clay or any other material. He used His words to create.

The Bible begins by telling us, "In the beginning God created the heavens and the earth. Now the earth was formless and empty, darkness was over the surface of the deep, and the Spirit of God was hovering over the waters" (Genesis 1:1–2).

Then God spoke, and when God spoke, things happened! There was light (Genesis 1:3). Then the sky. Dry ground. Plants. The sun and the moon. Creatures that swim in the sea and creatures that move about on land. And best of all, He created human beings in the very image and likeness of God himself. All of this is because God simply spoke!

There is a fancy word that people use to describe how powerful God is—*omnipotent*. *Omni* just means all, and *potent* means powerful. God is all-powerful. There is nothing too hard for Him! But God didn't just create all that there is; He is also involved in every detail of our lives. He is with us and working in our lives. So this great Artist, this powerful Creator, is our God, the only God, who made us and loves us and is always with us.

Action Step

Draw a picture or take a picture of something outside, something in nature. Share what it says about who God is.

Prayer

Father, we praise You for how beautiful and powerful You are. You are the Creator of all that there is. But You are also with us and for us. There is nothing that is too hard for You. Give us peace when we are worried or scared and remind us of Your strength. In Jesus' name, amen.

3

The God Who Knows All

Key Verses

You have searched me, LORD,
    and you know me.
You know when I sit and when I rise;
    you perceive my thoughts from afar.
You discern my going out and my lying down;
    you are familiar with all my ways.

Psalm 139:1–3

Key Idea

God is the only real know-it-all!

We probably all have a friend who seems to know it all! They might be very smart. Maybe they have a lot of facts or information memorized. Our friend probably gets good grades in school. And when we're talking, they think they are always right.

Now, having someone who thinks they know it all is not always a good thing! They can be wrong sometimes. If you disagree about something, they can be prideful. A friend can be rude or unkind and maybe not listen as they should. Even though they might be a great friend, sometimes all of that knowledge can get in the way of their actually loving and caring for another!

But here is the good news. God really is (and we say this with respect) a true know-it-all! And He is a GOOD know-it-all!

He knows all our thoughts. He always knows what is right and wrong. He knows the number of hairs on our head. The psalmist says He is "familiar with all" our "ways" (Psalm 139:3). He knows our fears and hopes and dreams. He knew when we would be born, and He knows the exact number of days of our entire life. "Nothing in all creation is hidden from God's sight" (Hebrews 4:13). He really does see all and know all.

And not only that, God is also full of love and compassion, and even humility. He listens. God is always patient with us. His decisions are never wrong. Whatever you are worried about, God knows about it. Are you arguing about something? He knows what to do. We don't have to be a know-it-all because God knows all! So we can trust Him and look to Him to always be right.

Action Step

Before you pray, share one thing you are worried about that you need to learn to trust God with. On an index card, write a verse to help you remember that God knows all things.

Prayer

Father, help us to be patient and kind to one another. Give us the strength to love each other and listen to one another. And most important, teach us to trust You—You are the only One who truly knows all things. So teach us to rely on You and trust You with everything in our lives. In Jesus' name, amen.

4

The God Who Is Everywhere

Key Verse

She gave this name to the LORD who spoke to her: "You are the God who sees me," for she said, "I have now seen the One who sees me."

Genesis 16:13

Key Idea

Wherever we go, God is already there.

Have you ever felt like you were all by yourself? Maybe you had to do something or go somewhere without a friend or your family. So you might have felt lonely. Afraid. Or even worried.

There is a story in the Old Testament about a woman named Hagar, who felt all alone. She was forced to leave her home and go live in the desert. A desert is a scary place! It's dry and dusty. It's full of dangerous animals. Worst of all, there are not too many people in the desert! It can be a lonely place. But Hagar discovered something really important about who God is. This is a reminder we all need.

As it turns out, Hagar was not alone. God was there. This is why she says in Genesis 16:13, "You are the God who sees me . . . I have now seen the One who sees me."

Here is a word to describe God being present everywhere: *omnipresent*. We've already said that God is omnipotent. *Omni* means all and *potent* means powerful. He is also *omniscient*—or all-knowing. But what Hagar discovers is that God is also omnipresent—present or with us everywhere and always!

No matter where we go. No matter what we do. God is there. God is everywhere! When we get up, God is with us. When we go to school or go about our day, God is there. When we are scared, God knows and is by our side. And even when we go to sleep at night, God never sleeps. He is with us and watches over us, even when we can't watch over ourselves.

Wherever we go, God is already there!

Action Step

Share one thing you are worried about or nervous about that would be helped with a reminder that God sees you and is with you.

Prayer

Father, thank you for the reminder that You are always with us. You are not only all-powerful and all-knowing, but you are with us everywhere. Help us to believe You are with us, even when we can't see You or feel Your presence. In Jesus' name, amen.

5

God Is Three in One

Key Verse

Therefore go and make disciples of all nations, baptizing them in the name of the Father and of the Son and of the Holy Spirit.

Matthew 28:19

Key Idea

God is relational, and He wants to have a relationship with us.

Do you like ice cream? If you have ever eaten ice cream, or anything cold, you have probably eaten it too quickly. It's hard to be patient and slow down when you are eating something so delicious. And what happens when you are eating or drinking something cold and yummy too fast? You got it—you get brain freeze!

As we read the Bible, learning about God can be like that. We learn about Him slowly. God doesn't tell us everything about himself all at once. We learn little clues along the way. Starting in the Old Testament and then reading the New Testament, we put together different truths about who God is until we have a complete picture of Him! Kind of like solving a mystery. Or like eating or drinking a tasty treat—we have to take our time and be patient as we try to get some big truths about God into our little minds!

We are going to give you another word that might make your head hurt; it might give you a brain freeze! Are you ready? It is the word **Trinity**. It is not a word found in the Bible, but Christians a long time ago started using it to describe what the Bible teaches about who God is. Trinity means three. And it describes how God is One (Deuteronomy 6:4) but also three in One.

The Father is God.

Jesus is God.

And the Holy Spirit is God.

They are not three different gods. God is One, but they are three distinct persons.

Does your head hurt yet?!

The Bible teaches that God is relational, and that love has always existed between God the Father, God the Son, and God the Holy Spirit (John 15:9, John 17:1, and John 15:26). It's like love just oozes out of the God who is three in One!

Here's the best part: Not only is that amazing about who God is, but He made us to be in a relationship with Him so that we could share in this love. We were made to be in a relationship, with the relational God, by our faith in Jesus, through the power of the Holy Spirit.

Action Step

Since God wants to have a relationship with us, what is one way we can show our love for Him each day?

Prayer

Father, thank you for sending Jesus to be our Savior. Holy Spirit, give us faith to trust in Jesus and rely on Him every day. Help us to know and experience more of the love You have as Father, Son, and Holy Spirit. In Jesus' name, amen.

6

God Is in Control

Key Verses

For in him all things were created: things in heaven and on earth, visible and invisible, whether thrones or powers or rulers or authorities; all things have been created through him and for him. He is before all things, and in him all things hold together.

Colossians 1:16–17

Key Idea

God rules and runs the world.

Who would you say is in charge of your house? Who runs it or makes the rules?

It might sound like fun to be in charge, but it can be a lot of work for a parent or family member! But not for God. Remember, He is all-powerful. All-knowing. And present everywhere. Nothing is impossible or too hard for Him.

He is a Father. But the Bible also describes God as a King. And what do kings do? They rule! Have you ever heard God called *Lord*? That is a way of saying God is in charge. Another way is to say God is *sovereign*. He is a ruler. King. The one who is in charge and in control of all creation!

This is exactly what God **has** been doing, **is** doing, and **will** always do. God is in control. He reigns and rules and keeps the world running.

The psalmist says it like this: "For God is the King of all the earth" (Psalm 47:7). In the New Testament, we read how God is holding "all things" together (Colossians 1:17). A good and wise and powerful king, God not only created the world, but He is present in it. He didn't make the world and then disappear! We might not always see God. Or feel God. But He is in control. He is always with us.

He knows our dreams and our plans, and everything we worry about. Because He is in control, His plans and purposes never fail. And we can always trust that whatever happens, it is because God knows best, and He really does love us.

Action Step

The next time you go outside and play, bring home one item that reminded you of how God is in control.

Prayer

Father, we praise You because You not only rule over the world, but You also keep the world running. You made us, and You know and control all the details in our lives. Help us to trust You and know that everything in our lives is being taken care of by You. In Jesus' name, amen.

7

God Never Changes

Key Verses

In the beginning you laid the foundations of the earth,
and the heavens are the work of your hands.
They will perish, but you remain;
They will all wear out like a garment.
Like clothing you will change them
and they will be discarded.
But you remain the same,
and your years will never end.

Psalm 102:25–27

Key Idea

**Everything in the world changes except
for the One who made the world.**

Everything in the world changes, doesn't it?

You buy a new pair of shoes, and then they get dirty. A new shirt gets wrinkled. How about a brand-new shiny bike or toy? Yep! It gets dented and scratched. It looks new for a while, but then it starts to look old.

Even creation, the world outside, changes. A day starts out bright and sunny. Then it gets dark. The sun goes up and then the sun goes down. The moon floats through the sky and then disappears. Flowers pop up in the spring. They show off their beautiful colors. And then, in the winter, they die. The grass looks so green, like a thick carpet, in summer. Then it gets dry, turns brown, and feels scratchy on your skin.

The psalmist in the Old Testament noticed this. He praised God for His amazing creation. He thanked God because He is like an artist. But as incredible as creation is, he also said that it changes! It will "wear out like a garment," or piece of clothing.

He also said something else. Something really important. Something we all need to remember. He tells us that God will never change! He writes, "You remain the same, and your years will never end" (Psalm 102:27).

Did you catch that? Everything changes. Clothes. Friends and family. Toys. The sun, moon, and stars. Your favorite pet. That new scooter. You name it—it changes! Except for God. He doesn't get tired. He doesn't grow old. He never gets sick. And because He is already perfect, He doesn't even get better! He never changes. He is *immutable*—a word that means unchanging!

Everything in the world changes except for the One who made the world. So we can always count on Him. He is the One who makes us feel stable and secure—and safe because He never changes.

Action Step

Share one attribute or characteristic about God that you are most thankful for that never changes.

Prayer

Father, we know everything changes except You. Keep us from looking to other things to make us feel safe or secure. And remind us that You are the One who never changes. Help us trust. Fill us with peace as You daily remind us that You remain the same. In Jesus' name, amen.

God Is a Shepherd

Key Verses

The LORD is my shepherd, I lack nothing.
    He makes me lie down in green pastures,
he leads me beside quiet waters,
    he refreshes my soul.

Psalm 23:1–3

Key Idea

God loves us and leads us.

We've already learned some big words to help us understand what God is like! Adults sometimes use different words and ways to describe how God is all-powerful, all-knowing, and present everywhere we go.

But did you know that in the Bible, it was common to describe God in a different way? God's people used images. Things they saw every day.

Try this out! Take a minute and close your eyes. What do you see when you think about God as *omniscient*, or all-knowing? Okay, how about this one: What do you see when you think about how God is *omnipresent*, or present everywhere? It's pretty amazing to think about, but maybe kind of hard to picture in your mind, right?

Now try this out. Close your eyes again. What do you see when you think about God as a shepherd? Or a rock? How about when you think about how God is like an eagle with mighty wings? Those "pictures" of God are a lot easier to see! That is another way the Bible helps us to understand who God is.

The psalmist wrote in Psalm 23, "The Lord is my shepherd, I lack nothing. He makes me lie down in green pastures, he leads me beside quiet waters, he refreshes my soul" (Psalm 23:1–3). Like a good shepherd, God protects and cares for His people. He knows us and looks after us.

In the New Testament, we read how Jesus is the Perfect Shepherd. He says about himself in John 10:11: "I am the good shepherd. The good shepherd lays down his life for the sheep." We never have to fear we are alone. Jesus loves us and leads us in every step we take. And He even gives His life for us!

Action Step

What comes to your mind when you think about God as a shepherd?

Prayer

Father, You are amazing. There are so many ways to understand who You are. Thank You for showing us what You are like by describing Yourself as our Shepherd. Continue to lead and care for us as we follow and trust You. In Jesus' name, amen.

9

God Is a Rock

Key Verses

I love you, LORD, my strength.

The LORD is my rock, my fortress and my deliverer;
    my God is my rock, in whom I take refuge,
    my shield and the horn of my salvation, my stronghold.

Psalm 18:1–2

Key Idea

God is our strength and our shelter.

Rocks are everywhere! If you were to take a shovel and pull up a scoop of the earth in a garden, guess what you would find—rocks! And of course, some mud and sand and maybe thick clay. Walk along the beach, and guess what you find—rocks!

In your front yard? Yep.

How about your backyard? There too!

Tiny rocks. Rocks with jagged edges. Rocks that are silky smooth. And rocks that are rough as sandpaper.

But guess where else there are lots of rocks—and we don't mean itsy-bitsy rocks. We are talking about huge, bigger-than-your-house, wider-than-a-semitruck rocks!

In the land of Israel.

The land where Abraham, Isaac, and Jacob pitched tents. Where God's people assembled a big portable tent, called the tabernacle, in the wilderness and then built a temple in Jerusalem to worship the LORD. Where David killed Goliath! Where Jesus lived and died and rose again. Okay, you get the point! Everywhere God's people went, there were rocks.

This is one of the reasons why in the Bible, God is described as not only a shepherd but also a ROCK!

"I love you, LORD, my strength. The LORD is my rock, my fortress and my deliverer; my God is my rock, in whom I take refuge, my shield and the horn of my salvation, my stronghold" (Psalm 18:1–2).

These rocks were enormous. Strong. Always there. And impossible to move. You could even hide in some of them. The psalmist probably looked around, spotted one of these, and thought, *That is what God is like! He is "my rock, my fortress." I take "refuge," or find safety and protection, in Him when I am afraid or worried.*

Think about that for a minute—everywhere God's people went, they were reminded of what God is like. Every time they saw a rock, no matter where and no matter what size, they could sing with joy that our God is a Rock who is strong and a shelter when we are in trouble!

Action Step

Find a rock that you can write Psalm 18:1–2 on. Put it somewhere you will see it every day!

Prayer

Father, You are our Rock. You are always there for us. Strong and sturdy. You are faithful. You are our hiding place and refuge. Remind us that we can run to You any time for help. In Jesus' name, amen.

10

God Is Eagles Wings

Key Verses

He shielded him and cared for him;
   he guarded him as the apple of his eye,
like an eagle that stirs up its nest
   and hovers over its young,
that spreads its wings to catch them
   and carries them aloft.

Deuteronomy 32:10–11

Key Idea

God can deliver anyone, anywhere, and in any way.

Birds are amazing animals. Did you know there are over 10,000 species of birds? They live in every part of the world. And come in all different sizes, shapes, and colors!

There are some birds (ducks) that sleep with one eye open.

There are birds that can't fly, like the penguin, but can jump really high!

Birds stick together, like good friends, in what are called flocks.

Hummingbirds are so light that they are like holding a nickel in the palm of your hand.

And there are huge birds, like owls and eagles, that can spread their wings as wide as nine feet.

As we have said already, the Bible uses pictures and images such as rocks, shepherds, and living water to describe what God is like. These images help us see who God is and what He does for His people more clearly. You probably guessed already another image the Bible uses to teach us about God—He is like a bird!

In the Old Testament book of Deuteronomy, the writer reminds God's people that God is like an eagle. That is a big bird you don't want to mess with! He writes this in Deuteronomy 32:11, "Like an eagle that stirs up its nest and hovers over its young, that spreads its wings to catch them and carries them aloft."

He is saying that God is like an eagle that cares for His people and "spreads its wings" to protect and deliver those He loves. He is swift. Strong. Protective. And able to deliver.

This is who God still is. He loves us and cares for us. He watches over us and spreads His wings to protect us. He can deliver anyone, anywhere, and in any way. So the next time you are afraid or feel alone, remember that God is like an eagle. He carries you on His wings (Exodus 19:4). He is watching over you, caring for you, and protecting you in ways you may not even see!

Action Step

Share one thing about a bird that reminds you of what God is like.

Prayer

Father, there is no one like You. You are strong and loving. And like an eagle, You are swift and able to deliver us. You care for us and are always with us. Thank You for all that You have promised to do for us. In Jesus' name, amen.

Created to Be a Friend of God

Key Verse

Then God said, "Let us make mankind in our image, in our likeness, so that they may rule over the fish in the sea and the birds in the sky, over the livestock and all the wild animals, and over all the creatures that move along the ground."

Genesis 1:26

Key Idea

You were created to be the best friend of the best Friend ever.

You have a friend. But not just any friend. You have the best Friend you could ever ask for! Who is that? You guessed it—God.

God, who is Father and Son and Holy Spirit, made you. You are not an accident. And you are not alone. The God who spoke all of creation into existence using His powerful word saved the very best for last. He is a Creator. But He created us for a purpose.

After He had made the heavens and the earth, He filled it with every living creature. But He wasn't done. He made human beings (the very first were Adam and Eve) *in His image*.

He didn't make angels in His image.

He didn't make dogs or cats in His image.

He didn't make kangaroos or penguins or porcupines in His image. He made YOU in His image.

We are truly unique, or special, in all of God's creation. He made us in His image and likeness so that we can be friends with Him. We can love Him, trust Him, obey Him, serve Him, and bring glory to Him in everything we do!

To be made in the image of God is to have emotions to feel and care about what God cares about. Being made in the image and likeness of God includes having a mind to think. It also includes having a will, so we can choose to love God the way He first loved us. As we grow in our friendship with God, we will look more and more like Him. Most important, we will love like Him!

We were made to be the best friend of the best Friend there is! And only this friendship with God the Father and Son and Holy Spirit can make us truly happy.

Action Step

Write down one way you can be a friend to others as God is a Friend to you.

Prayer

Father, You made us to be Your friend. Only in a friendship with You will we be happy. Help us to love You and to love others the way You love us. Fill us with Your Spirit so that we can continue to grow and look more and more like Jesus. In Jesus' name, amen.

The Saddest Day—
When Sin Entered the World

Key Verse

The LORD God made garments of skin for Adam and his wife and clothed them.

Genesis 3:21

Key Idea

**Even though Adam and Eve lost their perfect home,
they did not lose their perfect Father and Friend.**

Nothing new or perfect stays that way for long. Can you think of something that was new and began to fall apart?

That is exactly what happened with God's perfect creation. It's exactly what happened with Adam and Eve's relationship with God. And it even is what happened to their perfect home—the Garden of Eden.

Sin began to ruin everything!

First, Adam and Eve began to doubt God. They didn't think He was as good and loving as He said He was. Then they disobeyed God.

God had told them, "You must not eat from the tree of the knowledge of good and evil" (Genesis 2:17). Because He is good and loving, He had warned them that if they did eat the fruit, they would not experience the long and amazing life He had created them for. He was their perfect Father and Friend, but they would experience separation from God once sin entered the world.

That all sounds like really bad news. And it is. Unfortunately, that is precisely what happened after Adam and Eve ate the forbidden fruit. Sin brought pain, separation, and even death. For the first time, human beings knew what it was like to feel guilty, to know they had done something wrong. The way the Bible describes this is that after they sinned the "eyes of both of them were opened" (Genesis 3:7). It was an "OH NO!" moment. And they realized they were "naked"— which might sound funny, but it was no joke!

It means they knew they had sinned and were ashamed of it. And then they did what we have probably tried to do—they tried to "fix it" themselves. They tried to deal with their sin by making their own clothes, sewing fig leaves together.

That sneaky snake, the devil, had tricked them. (And as we'll see, the devil will be an enemy who keeps trying to keep us from loving God with all our heart!) Adam and Eve ran from God. They hid. And they blamed each other for eating the fruit. But here is some good news.

Only God can deal with our sin. Only He can fix the bad we have done. How did God do this for Adam and Eve? He would "cover" their sin by killing an animal and giving Adam and Eve clothes to wear from that animal's skin.

God was still loving them even though they had done wrong.

It was all a picture of what Jesus would do one day, when He would die for our sins. Like Adam and Eve's clothing, His blood would "cover" us perfectly and completely. Now when God the Father sees us, He doesn't see our sin, but He sees us "covered" in Jesus' love and forgiveness. The day Adam and Eve first sinned might have been the saddest day the world has known, but it was also a new beginning. It was a day when we would start to see just how deep and wide God's love for us is. And to learn how far God will go to love us, even when we sin.

Action Step

Write your own prayer today about why you are so thankful for Jesus' love.

Prayer

Father, thank You that You never stop loving us. We confess that we all sin, and we all need Your love. We need You, Jesus, to be our Savior. Continue to change us from the inside out through the power of Your Holy Spirit. In Jesus' name, amen.

Sin brought pain, separation, and even death. . . . The day Adam and Eve first sinned might have been the saddest day the world has known, but it was also a new beginning. It was a day when we would start to see just how deep and wide God's love for us is.

13

What's the Big Deal with Sin?

Key Verse

For all have sinned and fall short of the glory of God.

Romans 3:23

Key Idea

Sin is not just breaking a rule; sin is breaking a relationship.

What is the most important relationship in your life? Each of us has different relationships. Relationships with friends. Relationships with our parents and family. Relationships at school, on a sports team, or in a club. Relationships at our church. But the most important relationship we have is our relationship with God!

We've already said we were created for friendship with God. He is a Father and the best Friend we could ever ask for! But there is a problem—we don't always listen to Him or do what He asks us to, just like Adam and Eve. We do what we want. We say things or do things we know aren't right. And any time we choose to make something more important than our relationship with God, we are sinning. No matter how small or big—sin always hurts our relationship with God.

We all have "sinned and fall short of the glory of God" (Romans 3:23). God is completely perfect and holy. He is without sin. So sin is like missing the mark, or bullseye, of God's glory. But our sin is so much more than just breaking a rule. Remember, we were made to know God and to love and serve Him. We were made to enjoy Him and share in His love!

When David sinned in the Old Testament, he knew that sin was breaking his friendship with God. He once wrote and confessed to God:

> Against you, you only, have I sinned
> and done what is evil in your sight;
> so you are right in your verdict
> and justified when you judge.
>
> Psalm 51:4

David didn't want to do anything to hurt the most important relationship in his life. Sin is not just breaking a rule; sin is breaking a relationship. The good news is that when we sin, whether big or small, God is full of grace and love. When we confess our sins, He is faithful to forgive us and restore our friendship (1 John 1:8–9).

Action Step

Share one sin you need to ask God to help you overcome.

Prayer

Father, we are so grateful that even when we sin, You forgive us if we confess it to You. You want a closer relationship with us. So help us to see any sin in our lives that might be getting in the way of having a better relationship with You. Give us the power through Your Holy Spirit to love You as we should. In Jesus' name, amen.

14

God Keeps His Promise to Save

Key Verses

So the LORD God said to the serpent, "Because you have done this,

"Cursed are you above all livestock
    and all wild animals!
You will crawl on your belly
    and you will eat dust
    all the days of your life.
And I will put enmity
    between you and the woman,
    and between your offspring and hers;
he will crush your head,
    and you will strike his heel."

Genesis 3:14–15

Key Idea

Our sin might be great, but our Savior is greater.

We all make promises. Have you made one lately? Sometimes it is a promise to clean your room. Do the dishes. Walk the dog. Or maybe do homework. But we don't always do what we say!

God is not like that—He always keeps His word! The greatest promise He made was way back at the beginning of the Bible. It wasn't long after Adam and Eve had sinned.

Not only was God upset with Adam and Eve, but He was also really mad at that sneaky snake, the devil. God cursed the snake and declared judgment on him. He was not going to get away with what he did!

What did God promise?

A son. A Savior.

God promised that one day a son from Eve would win a victory over the devil. In Genesis 3:15, we read that a long fight would be going on between the son of the woman and the serpent. The serpent would "strike" the heel of the son, injuring him. But the son would "crush" the "head" of the serpent!

What was all this fighting and injuring one another all about?

A promise. Hope. Forgiveness.

Even in Adam and Eve's sin, God was offering hope. He was making a promise. Like a good Father, He was telling them that He still loved them, and He was going to save them fully in the coming of a son.

It would be His Son, Jesus, who would be born of another woman—Mary. Our sin might be great, but our Savior is greater! God's promise in the Garden was kept on the cross when Jesus died for us. And not only that, at the cross, Jesus "crushed" the head of the serpent.

Action Step

Share one way the devil is trying to keep you from loving God and others.

Prayer

Father, thank You for keeping Your promises to send Jesus. Even when we sin, we can know we have a Savior. Jesus has saved us and forgiven us at the cross. We praise You for winning this victory for us. In Jesus' name, amen.

15

Jesus Is Fully Human

Key Verse

The Word became flesh and made his dwelling among us. We have seen his glory, the glory of the one and only Son, who came from the Father, full of grace and truth.

John 1:14

Key Idea

Jesus became like us so that we could become like Him.

We use words to talk. Words to sing. Sometimes we use words to argue! Our words help us get to know each other better. We use words every single day to communicate. Have you ever wondered how many words you use in a day? It's probably a lot!

We've learned already that God talks too. He uses words. He created everything there is by simply speaking! Later in the Bible, in the New Testament, we learn that Jesus is called the Word. When God wanted to tell us and show us what He is like, He sent Jesus!

John 1:14 says, "The Word became flesh." In other words, Jesus became like us! He made His "dwelling among us," meaning that God wanted to be with us or live among us. All throughout the Bible, we learn how God loves to dwell or live with His creation. He lived with His people in the Garden of Eden. He dwelled among His people in the tabernacle (that portable tent God's people used in the wilderness). And in the Temple in Jerusalem. God loves to be close to us—which is why God would eventually come to us in the Person of Jesus!

Jesus had always existed. He was and is the second person of the Trinity. But when Jesus "became flesh," He became human.

Jesus had skin. Two hands and two feet. He got tired. Thirsty. Jesus' stomach growled because He got hungry just like we do! He cried when He saw someone hurting. He was happy. And He would even get upset when someone was hurting the people God the Father loved so much.

Jesus was fully human. In every way. Just like you! Now, He wasn't *just* human. We'll talk about that later. But He was **fully** human. He became like us to show us what God is really like. And He became like us so that we could become like Him. Because He was human, He knows exactly what we are going through!

Action Step

Take a minute and tell your family one thing you feel like you can talk about with Jesus because He was human.

Prayer

Father, You are so good and gracious. You loved us so much that You didn't just tell us what You are like, but You have shown us what You are like by sending Jesus. Give us faith to talk to Jesus about the big and the little things in our lives. In Jesus' name, amen.

Jesus Is Fully God

Key Verses

The Son is the image of the invisible God, the firstborn over all creation. For in him all things were created: things in heaven and on earth, visible and invisible, whether thrones or powers or rulers or authorities; all things have been created through him and for him.

Colossians 1:15–16

Key Idea

Because Jesus is God, what He says is trustworthy and true.

Wait a minute. Didn't we just say Jesus was fully *human*? And now we are saying Jesus is fully *God*? This is exactly what some of the earliest Christians were trying to figure out too! It is a mystery. And hard to understand. But it is something really important to know and believe—especially since Christians from the very beginning taught this about Jesus.

In fact, in AD 325, over three hundred church leaders, or bishops, met in the country that is now called Turkey to explain how Jesus is fully human AND fully God! It was known as the Council of Nicea. A council is like a big group meeting to discuss the Bible and what the church should believe.

As we said already, Jesus was just like us in His humanity. But because He was also God in the flesh, He was completely different from us as well!

God came to us in a Person so we could better understand what He is really like. Those first followers of Jesus could see Him. They could touch Him. They ate lots of tasty meals with Him. They went on trips with Him. And, of course, they had plenty of time to just be together, probably laughing and talking and discussing how amazing it is to love God and be loved by Him.

Jesus gave sight to the blind. He helped the lame to walk. By His power, He opened the ears of the deaf. He healed every disease and sickness. Because He was God, He forgave sins. He taught like no one else had or could. He even raised the dead. And most important, by His own death and resurrection, He defeated sin, Satan, and death!

Jesus was God in the flesh. And because He wasn't just a good teacher, prophet, or nice guy, we can trust Him. Everything He said and taught is true!

Action Step

Discuss what you think was hardest for Jesus about being God in the flesh.

Prayer

Father, it is hard sometimes to understand all that You have taught. Teach us and help us to understand just how amazing Jesus really is. Give us faith to trust Him because of who He is and what He did for us. In Jesus' name, amen.

17

Jesus Shows Us How to Live

Key Verses

Follow God's example, therefore, as dearly loved children and walk in the way of love, just as Christ loved us and gave himself up for us as a fragrant offering and sacrifice to God.

Ephesians 5:1–2

Key Idea

We will become like the person we are following.

Have you ever followed someone else? Or wanted to be like a friend, a favorite sports star, or singer? We will become like who we are following!

We can start to dress like them.

Talk like them.

Treat others as they do.

Everything about us can become like the person we are following.

This is why it is so important for us to follow the right people. And even more important, to follow the right Person—Jesus.

The very first disciples, or followers, of Jesus wanted nothing more than to follow Him and become more like Him. They wanted the life He was offering them!

One day, Jesus was walking along the shores of the Sea of Galilee, and He saw two brothers—James and John, the sons of Zebedee. He said, "Come, follow me" (Matthew 4:19). Guess what they did. They dropped everything. Left their fishing nets. And if you can believe this, they even left their dad sitting in the boat!

Jesus would teach them that following Him would be like being born again (John 3:3). Say what? This confused people. Jesus wasn't saying we had to crawl back into our mother's womb! He was saying that when you put your faith in Him, He gives us His Spirit to live inside of us. And it is like starting over. It's like becoming a new person.

Jesus calls us to be born again, and then He teaches us how to live again. How to *really* live! Over time, and with His help, He wants to change who we are—for the better. He wants to change us so we grow into people who love God and love others more than anything else.

Action Step

Think of one way you would like to be more like Jesus.

Prayer

Father, thank You for showing us how to live. You sent Jesus to be our Savior, but He also shows us how we can have real life. Continue to teach us to follow Him more closely. And give us the grace to become more like Him in everything we do. In Jesus' name, amen.

18

Jesus Died as Our Substitute

Key Verse

Look, the Lamb of God, who takes away the sin of the world!

John 1:29

Key Idea

Jesus didn't die for *His* sins but for *our* sins.

Have you ever had a substitute teacher at school? Maybe your teacher was sick or on vacation. So someone who was not your teacher filled in. They took his or her place. They were a substitute for the person who normally teaches!

It's kind of like what Jesus did for us on the cross!

At the beginning of Jesus' ministry and teaching on earth, John was near Jerusalem, baptizing people. He looked up, maybe squinted into the sun. Wiping the sweat and tears from his eyes, he saw Jesus coming! His eyes widened. His mouth probably dropped open in excitement. And finally, he couldn't keep quiet anymore. So he shouted to everyone who could hear:

Look, the Lamb of God, who takes away the sin of the world!

John 1:29

Do you remember from the Old Testament when God's people, the Hebrews, were in slavery in Egypt? God had commanded them to take a lamb and use its blood on the doorposts of their homes. God came to judge the Egyptians for rejecting Him over and over again. He used those ten terrible plagues! The last one was the most terrible of all. But He also promised He would "pass over" every home covered by the blood of the lamb (Exodus 12:13).

Every year after that, God's people would celebrate how the blood of a lamb had saved them. God had shown His power but also His grace. The yearly Passover celebration also pointed *forward* to the coming of a Savior—even if they didn't fully understand who that Lamb would be yet!

So this is why John was so excited. The real Lamb. The perfect Lamb. The final Lamb had arrived. He would die and shed His blood. He was a substitute for us. He took our place on the cross. And paid for our sins once and for all. As we'll see, this Lamb wasn't dead for long! He would die and rise again.

Why did Jesus die? Because He loves us. In the Old Testament, God had made a plan for His people to be forgiven when they sinned, which involved killing an animal as a sacrifice. Jesus was the perfect sacrifice, the Lamb of God, who loved us so much He was willing to die for us, so we could be forgiven and set free from sin! He didn't want anything to get in the way of having a relationship with us. Jesus didn't die for His sins; Jesus died for *our* sins!

Action Step

This week, write out John 1:29 on an index card, tape it to the bathroom mirror, and work on memorizing it when you get ready in the morning.

Prayer

Father, You loved us so much that You were willing to send Your Son, Jesus, to die for us. He was our substitute, taking our place on the cross. He died so that we can live, now and forever, with You. In Jesus' name, amen.

The Happiest Day—
When Jesus Rose Again!

Key Verses

Jesus said to her, "I am the resurrection and the life. The one who believes in me will live, even though they die; and whoever lives by believing in me will never die. Do you believe this?"

John 11:25–26

Key Idea

Jesus' victory is *our* victory.

It was the saddest day. A dark day. A scary day.

It looked like Jesus had lost. He had been arrested. Betrayed by His closest friends. Stripped of His clothes. The soldiers made fun of Him. They even took Jesus, beat Him, and placed a crown of thorns on His head. All of this He went through with courage and faithfulness, and love to die for our sins.

They led Him to a place called Golgotha, which means "the place of the skull" (Matthew 27:33).

His closest followers were "watching at a distance." Along with the crowds, they had heard Jesus say, "It is finished," then they watched as "he gave up his spirit" (John 19:30).

But the saddest day would lead to what would be the happiest day—the day Jesus rose again. It didn't come right away. They would have to wait. And wonder. But in just a few days, everything would change!

The Bible tells us that a man named Joseph of Arimathea came and took Jesus' body down from the cross. He wrapped it in a clean linen cloth and then placed Jesus' body in a tomb "cut out of the rock" (Matthew 27:60). It was a tomb Jesus wouldn't need for long!

Out of fear that Jesus' followers would steal Jesus' body and lie about Him rising again, the religious leaders asked that Jesus' tomb be sealed. They wanted it guarded with the toughest of the tough Roman soldiers! But these measures were no match for God.

On the third day, the ground began to shake. The stone rolled away. Life and light exploded. Death and darkness ran! Jesus was alive. He had risen. And His followers couldn't believe it!

Jesus' resurrection proves He really was who He said He was! He has defeated sin, Satan, and death. The grave is empty, and hope is alive. His victory is our victory. Just as Jesus rose again, we will also one day!

Action Step

Describe how you *feel* when you think about Jesus rising from the dead.

Prayer

Father, remind us that we have hope because of what Jesus has done for us. No matter what we go through, we can feel joy and peace. Thank You for the gift of salvation. Jesus has won a victory for us in His life, death, and resurrection. In Jesus' name, amen.

Chosen and Called

Key Verse

This is love: not that we loved God, but that he loved us and sent his Son as an atoning sacrifice for our sins.

1 John 4:10

Key Idea

We love God because He first loved us.

Have you ever been picked to be on a team? Maybe you waited, along with your friends, on the playground. You stood, hoping to get picked to be on a kickball team. Or for basketball or some other sport you love to play.

Two team captains stood and looked at the group. *Hmm,* they thought, *Who do I want on my team?* They thought about who was fast. Who could catch a ball. Who could throw a ball. Then, finally, they made a choice. One by one, the names of the chosen were called.

Did you know the Bible says you were chosen and called too? But it wasn't like a team captain looking at you and choosing you because you were good, fast, or strong! God looked at you out of His love for you and said, "I love you. You are mine. And I want You to know me and love me and be a friend, a child of mine." Long before you were born, even before creation itself, God knew you, loved you, and chose you to belong to Him by faith (Ephesians 1:4)!

We were chosen and called by God out of God's love (1 Corinthians 1:9). Like a magnet that tugs and draws objects to itself, it is God's love that pulls us to say **YES** to Jesus!

It's not because we are good. It's not because we are perfect. It's not because we have never sinned. It's not because we worked up enough strength to choose God. Or said enough prayers. Or read enough of our Bible. It is God's grace, His undeserved and unconditional love!

Here is one of the ways the Bible describes God's love: "This is love: not that we loved God, but that he loved us and sent his Son as an atoning sacrifice for our sins" (1 John 4:10). He loved us first. He took the first step. Made the first move. He sent His Son to die for our sins. And now everything we do in our life is meant to show our love for God. Our life is supposed to be our way of saying, "Thank You for choosing me and calling me!"

Action Step

In one word, describe how it feels to know that God chooses you and calls you.

Prayer

Father, thank You for loving us first. For inviting us to be friends with You. Even though we are not perfect or always faithful to You, You are so kind and gracious to call us, and You want us to be in a relationship with You through our faith in Jesus. Continue to change us and grow us by the power of Your Spirit. In Jesus' name, amen.

What Is Faith?

Key Verse

For we live by faith, not by sight.

2 Corinthians 5:7

Key Idea

God wants us to have faith in Him but also to be faithful to Him.

At night, everything is harder to see. And scary, too, isn't it? A creaky floor. Wind whipping and whining outside your window. A *thud* or *clunk* from a furnace heating your home. It all sounds like a big scary monster when you can't see what is making those noises!

Maybe you have played a game of tag or hide-and-seek after the sun went down! Or, have you ever been blindfolded and swung a stick or baseball bat at a piñata?

Whatever your situation, it is hard when you can't see clearly!

The Bible talks about how following Jesus can be this way. Sometimes in life, it can be hard to see what God is doing. Or maybe why God is doing something. You have to move to a new city. A parent takes a different job. One of your friends moves to a different town or city. Or maybe someone in your family gets sick. It can be hard to see the purpose or the plan God has.

So we need faith. We need trust. We need to believe what God has said to us in His Word, the Bible. It can be hard at times, but we must learn to "live by faith, not by sight" (2 Corinthians 5:7).

This type of faith-walking begins when we become a Christian—when we first put our faith in Jesus that He died and rose again for us! Have you ever done that?

That's where our life of faith begins. We have to turn from our sins (or repent) and turn to Jesus as our Savior. And then, as our Savior and Lord, He promises to always lead us! Our job is to have faith in Jesus but also to be faithful to Jesus.

When we follow Him and have faith in Him, we never truly walk in the dark. He has promised to NEVER leave us or forsake us (Deuteronomy 31:6)!

Action Step

How do you show each day that you have faith in Jesus?

Prayer

Father, give me the grace I need each day to have faith in You. Teach me to not just say I believe in You but help me show others by the way I live. We want to have faith in You, but also be faithful to You in everything we do. In Jesus' name, amen.

What Is Grace?

22

Key Verses

For it is by grace you have been saved, through faith—and this is not from yourselves, it is the gift of God— not by works, so that no one can boast.

Ephesians 2:8–9

Key Idea

God did something for us that we could never do for ourselves.

Who doesn't love to receive gifts?! Whether they are for Christmas, for a birthday, or from someone just being nice, everyone likes getting gifts. What is your favorite gift you have ever received? Who gave it to you and why?

A new shirt or sweater is pretty cool.

So is a toy. A bike. Or a gift card to your favorite store.

Those are all amazing gifts!

But the greatest gift we have ever been given is what Jesus has done for us on the cross. We are saved or forgiven because of a gift. That is what the word "grace" means. Grace is God's gift of love and forgiveness that we didn't deserve or earn. It was freely given to us by God.

This is what the Apostle Paul was saying when he wrote to a group of Christians living in the city of Ephesus. He writes, "For it is by **grace** you have been **saved**, through **faith**—and this is not from yourselves, it is the gift of God—not by works, so that no one can boast" (Ephesians 2:8–9, emphasis added).

Like any gift given to us, we can choose to accept it (say yes to it), or we can choose to reject it (say no to it). We say YES to God's gift of His Son, Jesus, by accepting Him as our Savior. It is "through faith." It is by believing that Jesus died for you!

When you believe in Jesus, you become a child of God—adopted into His family, the church. What an incredible gift! This gift that God gives us is something we could never do for ourselves. We can't earn God's acceptance by being good. Or working really hard. It's a free gift of God's love that we can choose to say yes or no to. Have you accepted God's gift by placing your faith in what Jesus did for you on the cross?

Action Step

Share how it makes you feel to know that God has given you the gift of His Son, Jesus.

Prayer

Father, help us to never forget the gift You have given us. Thank You for Your grace. Give us faith to believe in Jesus. He is the greatest gift we have ever been given. In Jesus' name, amen.

23

What Is Baptism?

Key Verse

Therefore go and make disciples of all nations, baptizing them in the name of the Father and of the Son and of the Holy Spirit.

Matthew 28:19

Key Idea

If we have "died" with Jesus, we have also been "raised" with Jesus.

Jesus and His followers, the apostles, never turned down a good question! Questions help us learn. And discover new things. Are you someone who likes to ask questions?

The Bible is full of people asking questions. People just like us. People who want to learn and grow so we can love God more!

One day, after a crowd of people heard Peter give a stirring sermon about how Jesus is the Messiah, or Savior, several of them asked a really important question.

As they listened wide-eyed to Peter preaching, the Bible says they were "cut to the heart" (Acts 2:37). In other words, they felt really sorry for their sins. And they knew they needed a Savior. They knew they needed Jesus.

Their hearts were cut so that their hearts could be filled up with God's love! (Romans 5:5).

But after they believed in Jesus, what were they supposed to do?

They asked an excellent question, "Brothers, what shall we do?" Do you know what Peter's answer was? He told them to be baptized! (Acts 2:38).

This is something followers of Jesus have been doing ever since Jesus gave His command to "go and make disciples" and baptize them (Matthew 28:19). Once we believe in Jesus, we are called to be baptized into Jesus and His family, the church.

Baptism is like dying and rising again! When we go under the water, we die to who we used to be. And then, when we come up out of the water, it is a picture of rising again with Jesus—to a new life, one lived for God!

Action Step

Take a moment and share why you think it is important to be baptized.

Prayer

Father, we give You glory for saving us through our faith in Jesus. This is truly the best gift. Teach us to continue to die to who we used to be and live for You. We want to love You more than anything else. In Jesus' name, amen.

What Is Communion?

Key Verses

And he took bread, gave thanks and broke it, and gave it to them, saying, "This is my body given for you; do this in remembrance of me."

In the same way, after the supper he took the cup, saying, "This cup is the new covenant in my blood, which is poured out for you."

Luke 22:19–20

Key Idea

Reminders help us to never forget God's love.

We all need reminders—ways to help us remember what is important.

We set an alarm clock to remind us to get up in the morning.

A family member might remind us to do our homework or chores around the house.

We write to-do lists to remind ourselves what we need to do each day.

We memorize Bible verses to remind us of who God is and what He has done for us.

But there is another reminder we all need. The most important reminder! One that has to do with food and drink. It is a reminder that originally happened around a table. But today, most of us do it at church during a worship service. What is the reminder?

It is Communion. The Lord's Supper. Some Christians call it the Eucharist. It is a time when we remember what Jesus did for us on the cross!

Shortly before Jesus was arrested, wrongly accused of things He never did, beaten, and mocked, He shared a meal with His closest friends. The disciples sat at a table with Jesus. Hearts pounding. Minds stretched to understand what Jesus was telling them. They didn't want to believe He was going to die, nor did they fully understand what He was saying.

So, as we read in Luke 22:19–20, "he took bread, gave thanks and broke it, and gave it to them, saying, 'This is my body given for you; do this in remembrance of me.' In the same way, after the supper he took the cup, saying, 'This cup is the new covenant in my blood, which is poured out for you.'"

Today, every time we eat the bread that represents Jesus' body that was broken for us and drink the cup that represents Jesus' blood that was poured out for us, we are reminded of how much God loves us! We are being reminded that we have been forgiven. And we are being reminded that we have hope because Jesus really did die for us and rise again!

Action Step

When you think about what Jesus did for you on the cross, what are you most reminded of or thankful for?

Prayer

Father, we praise You for making a way for us to be forgiven. And for making it possible to be in a relationship with You again through our faith in Jesus. Remind us often of how much You love us and help us never to forget You are always with us. In Jesus' name, amen.

25

Jesus Goes Back to Heaven

Key Verses

"But you will receive power when the Holy Spirit comes on you; and you will be my witnesses in Jerusalem, and in all Judea and Samaria, and to the ends of the earth."

After he said this, he was taken up before their very eyes, and a cloud hid him from their sight.

Acts 1:8–9

Key Idea

Jesus was not only raised to new life; Jesus reigns over all of life.

Not long after Jesus died and rose again, He spent forty days teaching about God's kingdom (Acts 1:3). He was trying to help people understand how amazing it is when we let God be in charge of our lives! He ate with His disciples. He explained His mission and the reason He had to die and rise again.

He was promising that we would not be left alone. And that even though His mission was done, ours is not! We have a job to do. Our job is to tell other people about Jesus—wherever we go (Acts 1:8). He was also explaining how He and the Father were going to send the Holy Spirit to help us.

But then He did something else. Something kind of surprising. And hard to understand. He left! In His body, He went up to heaven, like a great and powerful King being lifted up to His throne! As people were standing around listening to Jesus talk, "he was taken up before their very eyes, and a cloud hid him from their sight" (Acts 1:9).

Jesus was raised to new life after His death. And then, like a conquering King who had won a great victory over sin, Satan, and death, He *ascended*, or went back to heaven, to sit at the right hand of God the Father. He was raised. He now rules. And one day He is going to return!

So, what is Jesus doing right **NOW**?

He is our advocate (1 John 2:1)! He is on our side. Our friend, reminding us that He has forgiven our sins. Jesus is praying for you. Cheering you on. And helping you live out your purpose to help tell others about what Jesus has done for us.

Action Step

Share how it feels to know Jesus is your *advocate*, a word that means He's a friend who is always on your side.

Prayer

Father, we praise You for raising Jesus to life. Jesus is our King. He was crucified, resurrected, and now reigning. One day, He will return. Help us to keep our eyes on Him as our Savior and friend. In Jesus' name, amen.

26

The Holy Spirit Is God

And do not grieve the Holy Spirit of God, with whom you were sealed for the day of redemption.

Ephesians 4:30

Key Idea

The Holy Spirit is not just a power; the Holy Spirit is a Person.

Have you ever had to do something by yourself? What was it, and why was it so hard? You probably know this already, but God never leaves us alone. He doesn't ask us to follow Him in our own strength. He sends His Spirit to live in us. And as we'll see, the Holy Spirit is more than just power!

Do you remember one of those words we used earlier to talk about who God is? The one we said might make your head hurt? It is the word *Trinity*. As we said before, it is not a word found in the Bible, but Christians a long time ago started using it to describe what the Bible teaches about who God is. *Trinity* means three. And it describes how God is One (Deuteronomy 6:4) but also three in persons.

The Father is God.

Jesus is God.

And the Holy Spirit is God.

When Jesus lived on the earth, He promised that He and the Father would send the Spirit (John 14:16). He said He would not leave us alone, like orphans (v. 18). The Holy Spirit would come to live inside us. We would be a little sanctuary or temple (1 Corinthians 6:19). Holy and set apart by God and for God.

The Holy Spirit would comfort us. Help us. Teach us. Guide us and protect us. Give us strength. These are all things we'll talk about more in our next devotion. But it is really important to keep one thing in mind first—the Holy Spirit is not just a power; the Holy Spirit is a Person.

He is the third person of the Trinity. He doesn't have a body like Jesus had. But the Bible teaches us that He thinks and feels and makes decisions. He can even be "grieved" or feel sorrow when we do not love Jesus as we should. These are all things a person does!

He is not a "force" or an "it." He does give us power, but more important, He first gives us God's presence. He lives in us. And He is always reminding us that God loves us and that we are His children (Romans 8:16).

We are never alone. We have God himself living in us. Working through us. And always for us!

Action Step

What is one way you think you can grow a closer relationship with the Holy Spirit?

Prayer

Father, You have given us Your Spirit to live in us. Thank You for continuing to lead us, help us, and grow us through the presence of the Holy Spirit in our lives. In Jesus' name, amen.

The Holy Spirit Fills Us

Key Verse

Be filled with the Spirit.

Ephesians 5:18

Key Idea

Being a Christian begins with what Jesus did for us but continues with what the Holy Spirit does in us.

"POP!" The sound of the balloon exploding made our ears ring. *Oops, I thought, I guess I filled that one too full!* So I started again, watching as a flappy balloon got bigger and bigger, filling it just right this time.

Have you ever had to blow up a balloon? Or fill a glass with water?

The Bible teaches that God wants to fill us! He wants to fill our hearts with His Spirit! When the Apostle Paul was writing to a group of Christians, he told them not to be out of control. "Instead," he wrote, "be filled with the Spirit." He wanted them to be filled with the Holy Spirit so they could follow Jesus more fully and faithfully!

We become a Christian by believing what Jesus did for us on the cross, but we continue to grow as Christians by what the Holy Spirit does in us. The Holy Spirit gives us strength or power. He helps control our thoughts and desires. He helps us say no to sin. He comforts us and protects us. The Holy Spirit even gives us different gifts to serve others. And God fills us with His Spirit so that we may know His love for us (Romans 5:5).

Just as you might blow up a balloon, making it bigger and bigger, God wants to make your heart "bigger" with His Spirit. He wants to fill you with His life! So open your heart and let Him fill you. Give Him control each day by simply praying, "Come, Holy Spirit, and fill me."

Action Step

Begin each day this week by simply praying, "Come, Holy Spirit, and fill my heart today."

Prayer

Father, thank you for the gift of Your Son, Jesus, and for the gift of Your Holy Spirit. Fill us with Your Spirit so that we can love You and love others in even greater ways! In Jesus' name, amen.

28

Jesus Is Coming Back

Key Verse

For the Son of Man is going to come in his Father's glory with his angels, and then he will reward each person according to what they have done.

Matthew 16:27

Key Idea

We are working for Jesus as we wait on Jesus.

Days turned into weeks, and weeks turned into months, and months turned into years. Waiting. More waiting. And even more waiting!

Ever since Jesus first told His disciples or followers that He would come back again, God's people have been waiting! Like a friend waiting for a good friend. Or a family member waiting for another family member he or she loves. God's people have been waiting for Jesus to come back again.

Have you ever had to wait a long time to see someone you love? Usually, the longer we have to wait to see someone we love and miss, the more excited we are to see them when they finally come!

The Bible tells us that when Jesus comes back again, He will make every bad thing go away (Revelation 21:1-5).

There will be no more wars or fights.

People won't get sick or hurt or sad anymore.

He is going to wipe away tears forever.

And no one will die.

There will also be a judgment—a time when Jesus reveals who He is AND rewards what we have done.

As we have said already, we are forgiven through our faith in what Jesus has done for us on the cross. This is a free gift. But Jesus, when He was talking about coming back again, said that when He returns, He will reward us for what we have DONE!

When He came the first time, He came meek and mild. Humble. He came as a baby. He was wrapped in swaddling clothes. Placed in a manger. Imagine the God of the universe, who made everything, squeezing into a teeny-tiny body! That was the first time He came.

But when He comes again, He will come as a King, with the armies of heaven. Jesus will be riding a white horse, the Bible says. He'll have fire in His eyes. He'll be dressed in a beautiful robe. And on His head will be many crowns (Revelation 19:11–14). It will be bad news for those who don't love Jesus and have NOT been waiting on Him!

It's going to be good news for us. A great day. A day like no other. A day when we finally see Jesus, and He rewards us for working for Him and waiting on Him!

Action Step

Draw a picture of Jesus, returning and riding on a white horse.

Prayer

Father, remind us to never give up. As we wait for Jesus to return, teach us to stay focused on living for Him and loving Him more than anything else. In Jesus' name, amen.

29

A New Family

Key Verses

But when the set time had fully come, God sent his Son, born of a woman, born under the law, to redeem those under the law, that we might receive adoption to sonship. Because you are his sons, God sent the Spirit of his Son into our hearts, the Spirit who calls out, "*Abba*, Father."

Galatians 4:4–6

Key Idea

We don't just *go* to church; we *are* the church.

Churches come in all different shapes and sizes. Some are big, and some are small. There are churches with brick walls. Some have tall steeples on top, like arrows, pointed toward heaven. And there are churches with stained-glassed windows, churches with no windows, and even some churches that meet in homes!

But the ONE thing ALL Christian churches have in common is that they are built on Jesus! What makes a church is not where it is or what it looks like. A church is a church if the people there believe in Jesus and love Jesus.

And the church is not just where we go—we ARE the church! Where the Bible says the *church*, it means the Christian people. People like you. And us.

People who believed and served Jesus one hundred years ago. Followers of Jesus from one thousand years ago. God's people in Africa and Australia or Iowa or New York City. Christians everywhere, no matter where they gather, to worship Jesus!

Think of a family. A new family. When you put your faith in Jesus, you are adopted into God's family, the church. God becomes your Father. The Holy Spirit lives in you, always reminding you that you are loved as a son or daughter (Galatians 4:4–6). You get new brothers and sisters.

When we go to church, we go to worship God with the songs we sing. Or the instruments we play. We study our Bibles. Pray. Maybe even sit in silence thinking about how amazing God is. We listen to sermons or lessons in class so we can learn more about Jesus and grow closer to Him. We serve and help one another.

Church is like belonging to the best family there is—a family where we love God deeply and love one another sacrificially!

Action Step

Share one reason being part of a church is so important.

Prayer

Father, You call us Your sons or daughters. You have adopted us into Your family, the church. Thank You that You have loved us and accepted us, and have placed us into a new family. Give us the grace to love You more deeply and to love one another more sacrificially. In Jesus' name, amen.

30

A Bright Future

Key Verse

Let us hold unswervingly to the hope we profess, for he who promised is faithful.

Hebrews 10:23

Key Idea

God does not promise us a future without pain, but He does promise a future with His presence.

"Hold on tight," you have probably heard a parent say.

"Don't drop that."

"Be careful!"

You've probably wrapped your hands around the chains of a swing at the playground as you pulled back and kicked your feet toward the sky! You have gripped the handlebars of your bike as you took every twist and turn down a bumpy sidewalk. You've carried a ball. Or held on tight to something fragile, such as an expensive dish or cup.

"Hold on!"

There is something else we need to hold on to. Cling to. And be sure we never let go of. It's called HOPE!

The writer of Hebrews in the New Testament says we are to "hold unswervingly to the hope we profess" (Hebrews 10:23). In other words, we are not ever supposed to let go of our faith in Jesus!

So what is hope? Hope is assurance or confidence of the future. It is believing that everything God has said is true. We can count on Him. He is reliable. Trustworthy. And no matter what happens to us in life, God is going to be there for us in the future. We have a bright future. So we need to hold on to Jesus and keep following Him, even when it is hard!

God does not say we will never go through something scary or sad. He doesn't promise us a future without pain. But do you know what He does promise us? A future where He is present (Matthew 28:20). He'll be there with us tomorrow. The next day. He'll be there next year and the next year and the next year!

How do we know we have hope, and that God can be counted on? Because of Jesus' death and resurrection. We have hope because we know Jesus is alive! That was not just a story. It is true. He really did die for us, and He really did rise again.

You are not alone. God is with you right now. We have a bright future no matter what because God is with us and for us!

Action Step

Why do you think it is so important to hold on to hope?

Prayer

Father, we praise You because You are always with us. You have given us hope for a future with You. No matter what we go through, You will be there. You give us the strength we need every step of the way. In Jesus' name, amen.

Section Two

What Do I Want
My Child to BE?

What is different about me if I believe in God? This section is all about becoming the person God wants us to be! In the next thirty devotions, we focus on Christlike character and virtue. We'll get back to the basics of what we should know AND who we should *become*!

31

What Does Jesus Want Us to Become?

Key Verses

As Jesus was walking beside the Sea of Galilee, he saw two brothers, Simon called Peter and his brother Andrew. They were casting a net into the lake, for they were fishermen. "Come, follow me," Jesus said, "and I will send you out to fish for people." At once they left their nets and followed him.

Matthew 4:18–20

Key Idea

We are learning from Jesus and learning to be like Jesus.

All of us are following someone. Have you ever noticed the more you spend time with a friend, the more you become like him or her? It might be a friend at school. A family member. Or a favorite actor or actress in a show we watch.

We are being changed by who we spend time with!

Who you hang out with has a lot to do with who you become. This is why it is so important for us to be careful about the friends we choose. And as we have said, the best friend we can have is Jesus. He is the one we should let change us and show us how to live.

So, who does Jesus want us to become? He wants us to become like Him. One of the words Jesus uses is **disciple**. Maybe that is a new word or a confusing word for you. But a disciple is someone who is a student. Or a learner. Every Christian is a disciple. As Christians, we are learning from Jesus and learning to be like Jesus!

In Matthew 4:18–20, we read about Jesus calling His first disciples. Their names were Simon Peter and Andrew. They were two brothers who were both fishermen. They were just going about their normal day when Jesus showed up!

"'Come, follow me,' Jesus said, 'and I will send you out to fish for people'" (v. 19).

Jesus was inviting them to become students of His. Disciples. Jesus was going to show them how to really live. He would show them what was important and what mattered in life. In time, He would teach them what it looks like to have God in charge of your life!

So who will you let change you? Will you be a student or learner of Jesus? Nothing is better in life than learning to be like Jesus and living for Jesus!

Action Step

Share one way you can grow as a learner or student of Jesus.

Prayer

Father, give us a heart to love You more. Continue to show us how to learn from Jesus and learn to be like Him. Give us the grace and the power to change, a little bit at a time. In Jesus' name, amen.

Making Time for God

Key Verse

Very early in the morning, while it was still dark, Jesus got up, left the house and went off to a solitary place, where he prayed.

Mark 1:35

Key Idea

If we want to become like Jesus, we have to spend time with Jesus.

Jesus was busy. Really busy.

Everywhere He went, people followed. Big crowds and small crowds. Everyone wanted Jesus to do something for them. And, of course, Jesus loved to help people. He had compassion on them. He wasn't bothered or annoyed. He had the heart of God for God's hurting people!

Jesus performed all kinds of miracles. He opened the eyes of the blind and helped them to see clearly. Sound rushed into the ears of those who had been deaf. Legs that had been weak and crippled were suddenly made strong. With a word or touch, disease and sickness dried up or withered away. Jesus even raised the dead!

He did all of this and more because He loved people, and He wanted people to know who He was—the Messiah or Savior.

Jesus was always busy!

Have you ever felt really busy? Maybe you had a lot to do at school or at home or for a team you're on. It can be hard when you always have something or someone pulling on you!

But do you know what Jesus did not do, even though He was extremely busy? He did not skip His time meeting with God. Even when people were looking for Him and asking Him to do one more miracle, show them one more sign, or help them with one more thing, He was never too busy to get alone with God the Father.

Sometimes He would drag himself out of bed and even get up "very early in the morning" (Mark 1:35). He would sneak away. Get alone and be by himself. He would make time to be with God the Father and pray or talk. This time alone with God helped Him live for God.

If we want to be like Jesus, we have to make time to be with Jesus. He wants to grow us and change us, making us more like Him. So no matter how busy we might be, we should never be too busy to make time for God!

Action Step

What is one way you can make time for God each day?

Prayer

Father, show us ways we can make more time for You. Keep us from being too busy. And give us time each day when we can be alone with You to love You and learn from You. In Jesus' name, amen.

Praising God in Prayer

Key Verse

The LORD lives! Praise be to my Rock!
Exalted be God my Savior!

Psalm 18:46

Key Idea

The key to prayer is to keep praying.

When you get up in the morning, pray! Pray when you are getting ready and brushing your hair or brushing your teeth. And when you go play a sport or take a test, it's okay to pray. No matter what you do, where you are, or who you are with, you can always pray.

Short prayers.
Long prayers.
Funny prayers.
Serious prayers.
Prayers out loud.
Or silent prayers.

You can pray alone or pray with a group.

The important thing as a disciple or follower of Jesus is to keep praying. Not because you have to, but because you want to! We pray because we love God and want to grow in our friendship with Him.

We don't have to be an expert at praying or always use the right words. Sometimes we might say the wrong thing or fumble our words. God doesn't care! He loves that we love Him and want to spend time with Him, talking to Him as we go throughout our day.

So the real secret or key to prayer is that simple—keep praying (1 Thessalonians 5:17).

But what do we say when we pray? Well, one of the things we should always do when we pray is *praise* Him for who He is! We can thank Him. Tell Him how amazing He is. This is what the psalmist does:

"The Lord lives! Praise be to my Rock! Exalted be God my Savior!" (Psalm 18:46).

We can say things like:

"God, I love You."

"I praise You for loving me and saving me."

"You are always so good and faithful to me."

"We praise You, Lord, for always taking care of us."

These are all examples of praise! So as you go about your day, don't forget to keep talking to God. When you see the sun peeking brightly through the clouds, tell God how awesome He is. Or at night, when the sun is going down and it looks like the sky is glowing with fire, praise God for His beauty and power. Praise Him when you think about His love. Keep praying and keep praising God—He is worth it!

Action Step

Finish the following sentence: I praise God because _____.

Prayer

Father, we praise You for who You are and what You have done for us. We love You and thank You for saving us and always providing for us. Continue to grow our relationship with You. We want to know You more and to live each day for You and with You. In Jesus' name, amen.

We don't have to be
an expert at praying
or always use the right
words. Sometimes we
might say the wrong thing
or fumble our words. God
doesn't care! He loves
that we love Him and
want to spend time with
Him, talking to Him as we
go throughout our day.

Telling God You Are Sorry

Key Verse

Wash me clean from my guilt.
Purify me from my sin.

Psalm 51:2 NLT

Key Idea

**We don't have to hide our sin because God
wants to heal us from our sin.**

Have you ever had to tell someone you were sorry for something you did? Maybe you had to apologize for something you didn't do. We have all had to confess something to someone else at some point!

A broken window.

Words we blurted out in anger.

Something we took that didn't belong to us.

Not listening to our parents when they told us to do something.

Or maybe not speaking up when we should have.

All of us, at different times and in different ways, sin. Sin always hurts our relationship with God. It pulls us apart instead of drawing us together.

But the good news is that God is always faithful to us. He is a perfect Friend. He is always willing to listen to us and forgive us.

In 1 John 1:9, we read about this kind of love God has for us. John, who was one of Jesus' first disciples, was writing to a group of Christians—a church full of disciples. They weren't perfect. They, too, sinned. And so, they needed to be reminded that God didn't give up on them. Because of what Jesus has done for us on the cross, God will not leave us or stop loving us—even when we sin! God's Word says,

> If we confess our sins, he is faithful and just and will forgive us our sins and purify us from all unrighteousness.
>
> 1 John 1:9

When we make time for God each day and spend time praying to Him, another thing we should always do is confess our sins. We should tell Him we are sorry for anything we have done that has hurt Him or hurt someone else. This is what the Bible means by confessing our sins.

We don't have to hide from God. We *can't* hide from God! He already knows us and knows what we have done. Because God loves us so much, He wants us to confess our sins so He can forgive us and cleanse us of our sins.

Action Step

Think of one way you can remember to confess your sins.

Prayer

Father, thank You for always being willing to forgive us. Help us set aside time each day when we pray to confess our sins to you. Fill us with Your Spirit; help us to overcome those sins and to love You more. In Jesus' name, amen.

Taking a Peek into Your Heart

Key Verses

Search me, God, and know my heart;
   test me and know my anxious thoughts.
See if there is any offensive way in me,
   and lead me in the way everlasting.

Psalm 139:23–24

Key Idea

**Even though the power of sin has been
broken, the presence of sin remains.**

Most gifts come wrapped in shiny paper. A sparkling bow might sit on top. Or a gift might come in an envelope with a unique design and creative writing. But the real treasure and joy of a gift is what is on the inside! This is why we are so quick to peek inside and see what has been given to us.

As followers of Jesus, God has given us the gift of a new heart. A heart that has been changed by God. A heart that now loves God and wants to please Him more than anything. A heart that has been filled with the Holy Spirit. God himself lives in us.

But inside our hearts, we also still have sin and selfishness. Even though the power of sin has been broken, the presence of sin remains. So as we are making time for God each day, and learning to grow in our relationship with Him in prayer, there is something else we need to do. We need to take a peek into our heart each day. Or, as some Christians have said, we need to practice a daily *examen*, a heart check.

Have you ever had to look closely at something to see if it is okay? Maybe you were looking at a new toy—looking for any dents or scratches. This is what it is like to do an examen of our heart each day!

Why do we need to peek into our heart? So, we can see how we can love God and love others more! Each day, as we pray, we can ask God to "search us" and see if there is any "offensive way" in our hearts. Once a day, try practicing the three Rs!

- **REVIEW** your day.
- **REPENT** of any sins.
- And then **REQUEST** God's help to give you strength to love Him and love others.

Action Step

Share one reason you think it is so important to peek into your heart each day.

Prayer

Father, help us to love You and love others as we should. Search us and show us where we need to grow more. Teach us to stay close to You. And give us Your power to overcome anything in our lives that is holding us back from changing into the people You want us to be. In Jesus' name, amen.

Knowing God More

Key Verse

I want to know Christ.

Philippians 3:10

Key Idea

If we truly love God, we will want to know God more.

Some people know a lot about a favorite show. They can tell you all about the different actors and can give you every teeny-tiny detail of the story in each episode! Other people can tell you all about a sport they love. A subject at school they really like. Favorite colors. The best books. Their favorite clothing. Makeup. The list goes on!

What do you love? What do you know a lot about?

We were created to know God and love God and serve God. Nothing could be more important! We can know all sorts of interesting facts about friends, subjects at school, sports, or our favorite hobbies. But our hearts will never truly be full or satisfied or at "rest" until we know God and love God the most!

So how can we get to know God and love Him more?

As followers of Jesus, getting to know and love God is a lot like getting to know a good friend. We spend time together. We pray. We go to church.

But one of the most important things we can do each day is read our Bible. It's doing what you are doing right now!

As disciples or students of Jesus, **we are learning from Jesus and learning to be like Jesus**. This is what the first disciples did. And one of the things the Bible tells us is that the first Christians were devoted to God's Word.

When they met, they would spend time together in friendship with one another. They would pray. And they would break bread, or take Communion. They would also spend time studying God's Word (Acts 2:42). They wanted to love and know God more so they could serve Him! If we truly love God, we will want to know God more! Not just facts about God. Not just information. But we will want to know Him as we know a good friend we love and want to spend time with!

Action Step

What is one way you can work on knowing God better?

Prayer

Father, we want to know You and love You more. Continue to teach us and show us who You are through Your Word. Give us a hunger to love You, know You, and live for You. In Jesus' name, amen.

The Truth about Love

Key Verses

Follow God's example, therefore, as dearly loved children and walk in the way of love, just as Christ loved us and gave himself up for us as a fragrant offering and sacrifice to God.

Ephesians 5:1–2

Key Idea

True love is doing what is best for someone else.

Did you know that on a bicycle wheel, the center of the wheel is called the *hub*? This hub has all sorts of spokes attached to it. Some bikes have twenty, thirty, or even forty spokes connected to the hub! The hub and spokes are what keep the wheel together and keep it going around and around and around!

Your life is a lot like a wheel. You have a hub, or center. What is our hub? Well, it is not just a piece of metal holding spokes. Jesus says our hub should be our love for God and our love for others! And what are our spokes? Well, we could think of all the different relationships we have as spokes! Jesus said each of these relationships should be filled with love.

A new command I give you: Love one another. As I have loved you, so you must love one another. By this everyone will know that you are my disciples, if you love one another.

John 13:34–35

A relationship with our parents. A friend at school. Coaches. Teachers. Our relationships with a brother or sister. Maybe a pastor or friend at church, or a Sunday school teacher. All of these are like spokes on a wheel. The question is, *are these relationships connected to love?*

True love is not just saying we love someone. True love is doing what is best for someone else. As Jesus is changing us, He is making us more like Him. With God's help, we follow His example and "walk in the way of love" (Ephesians 5:1). We love others with our attitude, words, time, and even our stuff. Walking in love means living an "other-centered" life, not a "me-centered" one! How can you keep love at the center, or hub, of your life and love like Jesus?

Action Step

Share one way you can focus on others more than yourself.

Prayer

Father, help us to love like Jesus. We can't love in our own strength or power. We need You. So give us the grace to put others first. Use our thoughts, attitudes, and actions to show others Your love. In Jesus' name, amen.

Overflowing with Joy

Key Verse

May the God of hope fill you with all joy and peace as you trust in him, so that you may overflow with hope by the power of the Holy Spirit.

Romans 15:13

Key Idea

If you have joy on the inside, it will overflow on the outside.

Who is the most joyful person you know and why?

Think about taking a sponge and dipping it in water. The sponge soaks up the water like it is taking a big drink! But then, as soon as you lift up the sponge and hold it in your hand, what happens? The water begins to drip out. Ooze out. And if you squeeze it, the water really overflows!

That joyful person you know is kind of like a full sponge, and their joy overflows onto everyone around them.

The Bible says that joy comes from God. He fills us with joy (Romans 15:13). We can have that happiness no matter what is going on in our lives. Our joy comes from knowing Jesus and trusting Him. It comes from believing that Jesus died for us and rose again. And it comes from trusting that He is at work in our lives when things are going well and when things are going badly.

We're a lot like that sponge. What is on the inside will overflow to the outside. We can't fake joy, and we can't hide joy. It just comes out of us—we drip and ooze and overflow with the joy of Jesus. Or at least we should!

People see joy in our eyes.

They hear it in our laughter.

They feel it in how we treat them.

They know by our voice.

And they really know we have joy when they watch us walk through the hard stuff with a good attitude (James 1:2).

Do you struggle to have joy? We all do! But God wants to fill us with joy as He fills us with His Spirit. God wants to fill your heart with joy like water filling up a sponge. But then He wants us to be the kind of person that is overflowing with joy. So that others may know the joy we have in Jesus!

Action Step

What is one way you can live with more joy?

Prayer

Father, fill us with Your Spirit. Give us joy. Soak our hearts like a sponge. And help us to overflow with the hope and joy You give us. We want others to have what You have given us. In Jesus' name, amen.

Peace with God

Key Verse

Therefore, since we have been justified through faith, we have peace with God through our Lord Jesus Christ.

Romans 5:1

Key Idea

If we want to live at peace with others, we have to be at peace with God first.

God can put any relationship back together again. Sometimes a relationship can get torn apart or broken. But nothing is beyond repair with God's help.

There is no friendship that can't be fixed when God is the One helping us to love and forgive. And the most important relationship He wants us to have made whole is our relationship with Him.

Being a person of peace begins with having peace with God.

The Bible says we used to be "enemies" of God (Romans 5:10; Colossians 1:21). Before we had a friendship with God through our faith in Jesus, our relationship with Him was like a torn piece of paper. Or a broken piece of pottery. But God, who loves us so much, made a way for us to be forgiven. And for our relationship to be put back together again.

When the Apostle Paul was writing to Christians in the city of Rome, he said, "Therefore, since we have been justified through faith, **we have peace** with God through our Lord Jesus Christ" (Romans 5:1, emphasis added).

When we didn't love God or trust God or have faith in God, we were like enemies. We didn't want to serve God or obey Him. But all that changed when we put our faith in Jesus! We went from being enemies to being friends. And the apostle writes that we now have peace "through our Lord Jesus Christ."

We have peace with God—in the most important relationship we can have. We know for certain that we belong to Him as His son or daughter. We have been accepted. And we are loved. What kind of person does Jesus want us to be? He wants us to be full of peace. He wants us to have peace with Him and peace with others!

Action Step

Share one reason having peace with God is so important.

Prayer

Father, thank You for making peace possible with You through Jesus. Make us people of peace. Teach us to walk as Your friends and to love others in the same way You have loved us. In Jesus' name, amen.

Peace with Others

Key Verse

Blessed are the peacemakers, for they will be called children of God.

Matthew 5:9

Key Idea

**Living at peace with others means turning
down the heat in our relationships.**

The pot of water on the stove was getting hotter and hotter. We were beginning to make dinner, but didn't think about how high we had set the temperature on the stove.

Little bubbles formed in the water, and it looked like they were dancing on top of it. Then steam began to rise. And just when the water was getting ready to boil over, we rushed back to the stove and turned down the heat! We almost made a real mess—all because we weren't paying attention to how hot the stove was.

We can be a lot like that hot water on a stove, can't we?

We can get mad.

Say something mean.

Or feel sad when someone says something mean to us.

If we are not careful, we can stop loving one another. Stop being kind and forgiving to one another. Stop treating one another with respect and honor. We can get more and more upset. So instead of living at peace with others, we can become people who are like pots of boiling water!

We can boil over with anger. Or maybe pout. We can stomp off to our room. Sometimes we get upset and begin to pull away or stop talking to a friend or family member. But this isn't the kind of person Jesus wants us to become.

One of Jesus' messages was that if we let God be in charge of our lives, we will be "peacemakers." In Matthew 5:9, He says, "Blessed are the peacemakers, for they will be called children of God."

Someone who is a peacemaker is a son or daughter of God. They are taking the heat out of their friendships. They are kind. Gentle. Willing to forgive. If someone upsets or hurts them, they talk about it instead of just getting mad.

Just as we have peace with God, He wants us to live peacefully with others.

Do you have any broken relationships? Are there friends or family members you need to be at peace with? Don't wait for them to come to you—make the first move to be at peace with them (Romans 12:18)!

Action Step

On an index card, write the name of one friend you know you need to make peace with. Begin by praying for them each day.

Prayer

Father, change our hearts. Help us to be full of peace. Take the heat out of any relationships that are broken. We want You to be in charge of our lives. So create in us a heart that loves You and loves others. In Jesus' name, amen.

When Waiting Is Hard

Key Verse

Be completely humble and gentle; be patient, bearing with one another in love.

Ephesians 4:2

Key Idea

Patience is waiting without complaining.

What have you had to wait for recently?

We've probably all had to wait for something we really wanted or were looking forward to. We've waited for a birthday. We've waited for our favorite holiday. A delicious meal. Maybe we have had to wait to spend time with friends or family. Or maybe we could hardly wait because we were so excited for school to be over! And sometimes we must wait for others.

Being patient is not easy, is it?

When we are waiting, we can begin to complain. We might grumble. We get that scary look on our face—you know, the one when we squeeze our eyebrows together and wrinkle our forehead! We can pout sometimes. Or get restless and antsy. Instead of being kind to others, we can get pushy with our words.

But God doesn't want us to live like that! That is not the kind of person He wants us to be. God wants to change us and help us grow into being more patient—like Jesus. Becoming patient means we are learning to wait without complaining.

We are gentle and not demanding with one another.

We are kind when we don't get what we want when we want it.

We trust God and His timing.

We don't give up when things are difficult.

These are all examples of being patient.

The Bible says that as followers of Jesus, we should be "humble and gentle." We are to be completely "patient" with one another because we love one another so much (Ephesians 4:2)! And one of the best ways we can tell how much we love one another is by how patient we are with each other.

Do you have a hard time being patient when you wait on something or someone? Tell Jesus. Ask Him for His help. Just as He has been patient with us, He wants us to be patient in everything we do!

Action Step

On a card or piece of paper, write down where you need the most help being patient.

Prayer

Father, You are patient with us. You are not in a rush with us. You don't get mad or pushy with us. You are kind and gentle and loving. Teach us to wait without complaining. In Jesus' name, amen.

How to Treat Others

Key Verse

Be kind and compassionate to one another, forgiving each other, just as in Christ God forgave you.

Ephesians 4:32

Key Idea

Treat others the way you want to be treated.

It's easy to love those who love us. It's not hard to be generous when someone has given us a thoughtful gift. And it is not difficult to say something nice when someone has said something nice to us. We easily help others if they have helped us.

But what about when we are dealing with someone who is grumpy or grouchy? How about someone who is not nice or doesn't give back in the same way we gave to them? How about the person who is impatient? Or the person who knew we needed something and didn't help?

The answer is the same: We are to love no matter what! And the word the Bible uses to describe how we are to love them is the word *kindness*. Being kind means treating others the way we want to be treated. This is what

Jesus was teaching in Luke 6:31 when He said, "Do to others as you would have them do to you."

How do you want to be treated? We probably all want someone else to be loving, forgiving, and patient with us, right? We want someone to share or help us when we are struggling. We want someone to use words that build, not tear us down. We want someone to treat us with respect. And to encourage us. To pray for us and with us.

If that is how WE want to be treated, that is how we should treat OTHERS!

In the Old Testament, Jonathon said to his close friend David, "show me unfailing kindness like the LORD's kindness as long as I live" (1 Samuel 20:14). As we continue to grow and become who Jesus wants us to be, He wants us to show love to others by our "unfailing kindness."

Don't let your kindness fail! Let your love for others keep shining and showing through in everything you do. Whether it is a friend, family member, or stranger, treat them the way YOU want to be treated. Treat them with kindness!

Action Step

Describe one way you can be kind to someone tomorrow.

Prayer

Father, we praise You and thank You for Your unfailing love toward us. Continue to soften our hearts and open our eyes to ways we can show kindness to others. Help us to love others the way You love us. In Jesus' name, amen.

Choosing the Best Way to Live

Key Verse

Love must be sincere. Hate what is evil; cling to what is good.

Romans 12:9

Key Idea

Goodness is doing what is right, even when it is not easy.

Have you ever built something?

With our cooperation, God is building us into who He wants us to be. The Holy Spirit, God himself, lives inside of us and is changing us. But God asks us to work with Him— to say yes to Him. And so, every choice we make is making us!

When we choose to love, we become more loving.

When we choose to be full of joy, we become more joyful.

When we choose peace, we become peacemakers.

When we choose patience and kindness, we become gentler with others.

Do you know what else God wants to build in us? **Goodness!** Being good isn't just about keeping rules or staying out of trouble. Doing good is living the way God wants us to. And it means doing what is right, even when it is not easy.

God wants good for us. But doing good requires choices every day!

We need to know what God's Word says. To surround ourselves with the right kind of friends. To spend time each day with Jesus. And with God's help, we then must choose to do good.

We need to choose what is good when our parents ask us to listen to them.

We need to choose what is good when we are watching a movie or listening to music.

We need to choose what is good when we are hanging out with friends.

We need to choose what is good when we are all alone.

Romans 12:9 reminds us that as Christians, we have to "cling to what is good." There are many things, and even people, trying to pry us away from doing good. So we must cling to doing what is right. We must cling to listening to God and pleasing Him more than pleasing other people!

What kind of life are you letting God build in you? Are you building love, joy, peace, patience, kindness, and GOODNESS? The Holy Spirit wants you, as a follower of Jesus, to live with goodness. This can be hard. So remember, do what is right, even when it is not easy.

Action Step

Share how and when you can do good for someone this week.

Prayer

Father, build us into the people You want us to be. Give us the power to do what is right, even when it is hard. Help us to love and live for You in all that we do. In Jesus' name, amen.

44

A Person Who Keeps Going

Key Verse

Now it is required that those who have been given a trust must prove faithful.

1 Corinthians 4:2

Key Idea

**Being faithful is sticking with someone you
love or something you are doing.**

Are you a "sticky" person? And we don't mean sticky as in you just put your hand on a plate of hot pancakes covered in maple syrup! We mean sticking with someone or something.

A sticky person is a faithful person!

Being sticky is being a loyal friend. Someone who is always faithful and devoted to a friend no matter what. They are there in the good times and in the bad times. A **faithful** friend is a dependable friend. They are always there.

Or being sticky can mean completing a job or task or homework. It means not cutting any corners or giving up because something is too hard or frustrating! A faithful person works hard without complaining. They are on time and listen to instructions. They do everything, big or small, like they are serving God.

That is the kind of stickiness Jesus is looking for in His followers!

Being faithful is the opposite of quitting.

In the Old Testament, one of the leaders of God's people was a man named Samuel. Toward the end of his life, Samuel gathered the Israelites together. He had an important message for them. He knew that God's people were kind of hot and cold.

There were times when they were faithful to God. They would stick to what God said. And then there were lots of times when they were unfaithful. They disobeyed the commandments and did what they wanted to do. So Samuel wanted to make sure they were sticky! He said to them, "But be sure to fear the Lord and serve him faithfully with all your heart; consider what great things he has done for you" (1 Samuel 12:24).

"Don't give up," he was saying. "Think about all that God has done for you. Serve Him. Stick with Him. Never give up. Be faithful because God has been faithful to you!"

How is God calling YOU to be faithful, or sticky?

Action Step

Share one way you can grow in sticking with a friend or a task.

Prayer

Father, we worship You because of Your faithfulness. Thank You for never giving up on us, even when we sin. Teach us to be faithful and devoted to You. Change us by the power of Your Spirit, so we do everything like we are serving You. In Jesus' name, amen.

45

Are You Prickly or Gentle?

Key Verse

Therefore, as God's chosen people, holy and dearly loved, clothe yourselves with compassion, kindness, humility, gentleness and patience.

Colossians 3:12

Key Idea

**Gentleness is being careful with others,
so they are comfortable with us.**

We're careful with things we love. Careful with things that can easily be broken. And careful with things that are valuable to us. But how careful are we with others?

In Colossians 3:12, we are reminded to be people who are growing in "**gentleness**." As God's people, we are to "clothe" ourselves with "compassion, kindness, humility, gentleness and patience." And in Ephesians 4:2, we discovered that God wants us to be "completely humble and gentle." Not a little bit gentle, but "completely" gentle!

Being gentle with one another is remembering to always be careful with those we love. How can we grow in gentleness? Here are a few practical ways we can all grow in gentleness:

- Pay attention to how others are feeling.
- Notice what they need.
- Ask yourself, *Is the person I am talking to comfortable and at ease?*
- Treat others with kindness.
- Use words that build up instead of tear down.
- Be slow to anger.
- Always use the best manners in what you are saying or doing.

Can you think of other ways to be gentle?

One of the best ways we can grow in gentleness is to remember that Jesus is gentle. Is this how you think of Jesus? Or do you think He is always upset with you or disappointed? Jesus loves us and is always inviting us to remember His love.

He is careful with us. Slow to anger and full of grace. He knows we are growing, so He is patient with us. He is not in a rush. And He is definitely not pushy with us! He is gentle, taking His time to teach us and allow us to be changed by the Holy Spirit.

Here's what Jesus says about himself in Matthew 11:29: "Take my yoke upon you and learn from me, for I am **gentle** and humble in heart, and you will find rest for your souls."

Since this is how Jesus is with us, let's treat others in the same way! The God who is always and completely gentle with us wants us to be gentle with others.

Action Step

Name someone in your life you should treat gently.

Prayer

Father, remind us that You are patient, kind, and gentle with us. You don't rush us as we grow into who You want us to be. Help us to be gentle with others, to be careful with those we love and make them comfortable with us. In Jesus' name, amen.

Building Strong Walls

Key Verse

Like a city whose walls are broken through is a person who lacks self-control.

Proverbs 25:28

Key Idea

**Self-control is the power from God to
think and do what pleases God.**

When we don't have self-control, we can be dangerous to others and dangerous to ourselves. And most important, when we lack self-control, we are not thinking or doing things that please God.

People with no self-control might speak without thinking about what their words will do to someone else. When we lack self-control, we let our emotions rule us. Or maybe our lack of self-control affects what we eat. Instead of eating foods that are healthy for us, we eat junk food. Without self-control, we will watch whatever shows or movies we want to, instead of thinking about what is right and what would honor God.

This is why the Old Testament tells us that a person who lacks self-control is like a city with no walls! They are at risk of great danger: "Like a city whose walls are broken through is a person who lacks self-control" (Proverbs 25:28). In the ancient world, walls were built to protect people.

If the walls of a city were strong and sturdy, enemies couldn't get in and destroy the city. Cities needed walls made of stone. And those walls were guarded by soldiers. When the walls were strong, the city was safe.

That is how self-control works in our lives. Self-control protects us. And it protects others. Every day, it seems, we face difficult decisions. It can be hard to live for God. So we need His help to give us the power to say no to sin and yes to pleasing Jesus.

The Holy Spirit, who lives inside us, can give us that strength. We simply need to ask. And to pray often, "Help me have the power to please Jesus." Remember, God knows what is best for us. He wants us to be like that city with secure walls. He wants to protect us from making bad decisions or doing things that will hurt us and hurt others.

Trust Him. Listen to Him. Seek to obey Him. Ask Him to give you the power you need to live with self-control!

Action Step

Share one area where you know you need to have more self-control.

Prayer

Father, we need Your power. Fill us with Your Spirit. Make us like a city with safe and secure walls. Show us how to live with greater self-control so You protect us and so we can please You in all we do. In Jesus' name, amen.

47

Learn and Then Live

Key Verse

The fear of the LORD is the beginning of wisdom, and knowledge of the Holy One is understanding.

Proverbs 9:10

Key Idea

Wisdom is skilled living.

Do you know someone who is really good at something? What is it, and who are they?

You might have a friend who is good at playing basketball. Or music. Maybe you have a friend who rocks at video games. Skateboarding. Painting or drawing.

Whatever it is, we would say that friend or family member is *skilled*. They don't just have lots of knowledge about music or a sport or hobby; they are good at it! They have learned, over time, to do it well.

Can you guess where God wants us to be most skilled? It's at living! He wants us to make good choices. Wise choices. Smart choices.

God wants us to be wise, or skilled, in how we talk to one another. Wise in the friends we choose. He wants us to be wise with our time and our stuff. And with the shows or video games we choose to watch or play.

This is what the word *wisdom* in the Bible means. Wisdom is skilled living. It's not just knowing what the Bible says. Or knowing what is right or wrong. With God's help, wisdom is making the right choices to live for God. It is being skilled, instead of being foolish, at living!

Proverbs 9:10 says, "The fear of the Lᴏʀᴅ is the beginning of wisdom, and knowledge of the Holy One is understanding."

"The fear of the Lord" does not mean being scared of God—it is loving God and wanting to please Him in all we do. That is where wisdom begins: with a desire to love Him and live for Him. Foolish people want to live for themselves. To do what they want to do. And this always leads to trouble.

The promise from God is that wisdom always leads to good things. Bad choices result in bad consequences, but good choices lead to good consequences. So don't just "live and learn," as the saying goes. God wants us to be skilled at living, so that we not only know what is right, but do what is right!

Action Step

Discuss one way you can grow in becoming wise.

Prayer

Father, You are the One who gives us wisdom. What You say is right and true. Living for You is the best way to live. Help us to be skilled at living life Your way instead of our way. In Jesus' name, amen.

A Heart of Justice

Key Verse

And what does the Lord require of you? To act justly and to love mercy and to walk humbly with your God.

Micah 6:8

Key Idea

Justice is giving others what they deserve.

At the very beginning of the Bible, we read that each of us is made in the image of God (Genesis 1:26–27). This means that every person— our friends, family members, neighbors, a stranger on the street— is loved and created by God.

Every human being is of incredible worth, value, and dignity. Every human being is worthy of our attention, time, and love. This is what it means to walk in **justice**. It is to see others for who they really are—and then to treat them in a way they deserve!

Has someone ever treated you in an unkind way or hurt your feelings? Maybe you feel they didn't help you when you needed them to, or they didn't listen when you were talking. You didn't feel loved or cared for. These are just a few examples of what it is like to be treated in an unjust way, in a way you didn't deserve.

In the Old Testament book of Micah, God told His people how He wanted them to live. He gave a simple instruction of how we should see and treat everyone. Here is what He said through the prophet Micah: "And what does the LORD require of you? To **act justly** and to love mercy and to walk humbly with your God" (Micah 6:8).

What does the Lord want from us? He wants us to "act justly." This is always how Jesus treated people. He wasn't rude or pushy. He didn't get annoyed. He gave to people. Listened to people. Met their needs.

As Jesus is changing us by His Spirit, He wants us to grow in justice. He wants us to see people differently. To treat them, no matter who they are, with kindness, love, and respect. God wants us to treat people with equality, not playing favorites! He wants us to be just and to give each person what they deserve. They matter to God, so they should matter to us!

Action Step

On an index card, write out Micah 6:8 to memorize this week.

Prayer

Father, we love You and worship You. Give us eyes to see people for who they really are. Soften our hearts so we can treat everyone with justice. We want to honor You and others by treating those around us with worth and dignity. In Jesus' name, amen.

49

Overcoming Fear

Key Verse

But the angel said to her, "Do not be afraid, Mary; you have found favor with God."

Luke 1:30

Key Idea

Do what is right, even if it is hard.

When was the last time you were afraid? What was it, and why did it make you scared?

It doesn't matter how old you are—we face fears every single day, don't we? It might be a friend or family member who is sick. Maybe it is a big test or a new class. We can fear what others think of us. Or we can be afraid of the future. Being afraid is normal, but it is not healthy! Instead of fearfulness, God wants to help build a different characteristic in us. He wants us to have *courage*.

So, what is courage, and why is it important?

Courage is doing what is right or good, even when it is hard. Or when it is scary! One example of having courage is found in Luke 1:29–30. This is the story of the angel Gabriel coming to Mary to tell her she is going to give birth to a son. And not just any son! Through the power of the Holy Spirit, she will give birth to Jesus.

And guess how she responds? She is afraid! How do we know this? As we read in Luke 1:30, the angel tells her to have courage. It says, "Do not be afraid, Mary; you have found favor with God" (Luke 1:30).

Mary would have had many reasons to be afraid, but the courage God gave her would help her say yes to whatever God wanted! In fact, in verse 38, Mary says, "I am the Lord's servant." In other words, she was willing to obey God and do what He wanted, even though she was afraid.

Having courage doesn't mean we aren't afraid. It means that even when we are afraid, we still do what is right or good. We trust God. We love Him more than we care about what others think of us. So where do you need courage most right now? Maybe it is to invite a friend to church. Or maybe it is to speak up for someone who is not being treated very well. Whatever it is, keep walking with Him even when it is difficult.

Action Step

Name something that makes you feel afraid and ask God to help you live with courage in facing it.

Prayer

Father, give us the strength to do what is right. When we are afraid, help us to trust You and to keep being faithful. You love us and You are always with us. In Jesus' name, amen.

50

Working Hard

The LORD God took the man and put him in the Garden of Eden to work it and take care of it.

Genesis 2:15

Key Idea

Our work is meant for loving God and loving others.

"I quit!"

Have you ever said those words? When God first created Adam and Eve, He gave them a job. He gave them work to do—work that was good, but probably not always easy.

God placed them in the perfect garden—the Garden of Eden. A home where there was no sin. No fighting. No complaining. There was no sadness or death or pain or suffering. Even in the paradise that God created for Adam and Eve to enjoy, they had work to do!

Adam and Eve's job was to help care for God's creation.

Work was not a chore. It wasn't something bad or boring or bothersome. Work was good. Their job had a purpose and was full of meaning. And just like Adam and Eve, we have work that is meant to be good too. We were created to work with God and for God. Whatever we do, we are to work hard at it. We are meant to love God and love others through our work.

Homework.

Doing the dishes.

Folding laundry.

Helping a brother or sister clean a bedroom, kitchen, or family room.

Helping your mom or dad pull weeds in the garden.

No matter what the task is, God wants us to become people who work hard. He doesn't want us to complain or quit or cut corners. He wants us to take joy in work. To have a good attitude in what we say and how we act.

Work isn't about becoming famous or getting rich. It's not about getting something done and just getting it out of the way! When we work hard, we are serving others and honoring God.

So how do you respond when someone asks you to do something? Are you someone who works hard to love and bless others?

Action Step

Share one way you can work hard to love others.

Prayer

Father, change how we see work. Help us not to complain or have a bad attitude. Give us a heart that wants to work hard and love others. We want to please You no matter what we do. In Jesus' name, amen.

Becoming Teachable

Key Verse

Get wisdom, get understanding; do not forget my words or turn away from them.

Proverbs 4:5

Key Idea

A teachable heart is open to listening and learning from others.

Learning something new can be fun and exciting. But learning something new can also be hard and frustrating, can't it? It takes time. And as we'll see, it takes the right kind of heart to learn and listen to others.

We are ALL learners! We are taught something new and different almost every day. What have you learned recently? Who taught you?

Someone taught you to tie your shoes. To use good manners. To work the TV remote. Someone helped us learn how to walk, feed ourselves, and understand a subject at school. We need teachers for just about everything—which means we also need to learn how to be taught. In other words, we need to grow to be a person who is teachable.

A teachable heart is open to listening and learning from others. This is what Jesus' first disciples had to be—***teachable***. They, too, were learning from Jesus and learning to be like Him. They weren't just learning a hobby or sport or how to do math. They were learning how to let God be in charge of their lives! So they needed to have the right heart to become a person who loves God and others.

An unteachable heart shows when we don't listen to other people's advice or wisdom. We argue. Complain. We think and act as though we always know better. Maybe a parent or friend tries to help us by telling us something, and we act stubborn or prideful. That is not how God wants us to be! And it is not what helps us grow, change, and experience all God wants for us.

The book of Proverbs reminds us that we all need help learning. We need to "get wisdom, get understanding" (Proverbs 4:5). We need to be taught by God and by others.

A teachable heart is open, not closed. It is open to learning and listening, growing and changing! Do you have that kind of heart?

Action Step

Share one way you can become more teachable.

Prayer

Father, teach us to have an open heart. A heart that is willing to listen to You and to learn from others. Give us hearts that want to grow and become who You want us to be. In Jesus' name, amen.

Taking the Fear out of Honesty

Key Verse

Therefore each of you must put off falsehood and speak truthfully to your neighbor, for we are all members of one body.

Ephesians 4:25

Key Idea

A person who is honest says and does what is true.

Have you ever played the game hide-and-seek? As you probably already know, the goal of that game is not to be seen! You don't want anyone to find you, hear you, or know where you are.

It's okay to do that in a game, but not in real life!

Do you know who you can never hide from? If you said God, you are right! Remember when we talked about God being all-knowing, or omniscient? We said that meant that there is nothing He doesn't know or see. "Nothing in all creation is hidden from God's sight," Hebrews 4:13 says.

At the beginning of the Bible, Adam and Eve tried to hide from God! They doubted that God was really good and that He wanted what was best for them, so they did what they were NOT supposed to do. They ate fruit from the tree of the knowledge of good and evil. Then they lied about it!

Instead of being honest about what they had done, they hid. They blamed one another. They turned away from telling the truth and walking in the truth. As followers of Jesus who the Holy Spirit is changing, we are called to "put off falsehood and speak truthfully" to one another (Ephesians 4:25).

This means we tell the whole truth, not just parts of it. When we make a mistake or do something wrong, we confess it, or tell someone. We have the courage to speak up for what is right, even if it is not popular. We don't keep quiet if we feel unsafe or uncomfortable. We don't exaggerate or try to make ourselves look better.

And most important, we never try to hide from God! Why? Not just because He sees everything anyway, but because He loves us and has forgiven us by our faith in Jesus. He doesn't want us to hide from Him and pretend we are okay when we aren't. Like a good Father, He wants us to come to Him and share everything with Him. You are His child!

Action Step

Why is it so important to be honest with God?

Prayer

Father, remind us of why we need to come to You with the good and the bad. Help us know we are safe with You and need Your love. Give us the strength to be honest with You and with one another. In Jesus' name, amen.

Grounded in Gratefulness

Key Verse

Give thanks in all circumstances; for this is God's will for you in Christ Jesus.

1 Thessalonians 5:18

Key Idea

**Thankfulness is living with a grateful heart for
who God is and all that He has given us.**

Who are you most thankful for? Is there something you have or something someone has done for you that you are really thankful for?

One of the simplest ways to find out how thankful we really are is to listen to how we talk or what we talk about.

A heart that is unthankful shows in

- Complaining: "Ugh, I don't want to go there or do that."
- Always wanting more: "I wish I had a new phone" (or those new shoes or that toy).
- Putting others down instead of encouraging others and saying how much we appreciate them.

- Rarely expressing thanks: "Thank you for taking me to the store." Or "Thank you for this dinner."

Our speech often shows whether we are thankful or unthankful.

We can learn a lot about our own hearts by listening to what we say or don't say! But when God is changing our hearts, we become more thankful. We live with a grateful heart for who God is and all that He has given us. **A thankful heart focuses on what it has and not on what it doesn't have!**

In 1 Thessalonians 5:18, we are told to "give thanks in all circumstances." Did you catch that? God doesn't want us to be thankful only sometimes. He doesn't want us to give thanks just when things go right. Or when we get what we want. To follow Jesus and be changed by Him is to grow into being thankful in *all* circumstances.

This is not easy, is it? We need God's help—His grace. We can become more thankful by starting with God and remembering why we are grateful to Him and for Him. We could take a journal or blank piece of paper and write down all the reasons. Or we can list all the things we have in our life that we don't deserve. Most important, we can pray each day, asking the Holy Spirit to help us live with a grateful heart for who Jesus is and all He has given us!

Action Step

Name three things you are thankful for today.

Prayer

Father, You have done so much for us. Give us hearts that are thankful. Help us to see who You are and what You have done for us. And teach us to be thankful for what we have and who You have placed in our life. In Jesus' name, amen.

54

Give Me a Clean Heart

Key Verse

Create in me a pure heart, O God, and renew a steadfast spirit within me.

Psalm 51:10

Key Idea

A pure heart is a clean heart that wants to live to please God.

Winter can be cold and dark. All the beautiful colors of spring, summer, and fall go into hiding. Gone are the days of blooming flowers and colorful leaves. Everything can look kind of brown and bare. Sort of dirty, and even ugly!

But then something happens. Snow begins to fall. It's like someone takes a pillow full of soft white cotton and rips it open. The fluffy snowflakes fall to the ground, covering the dirt, the dead grass, and the tree limbs.

The snow makes everything look and feel bright. Clean. And beautiful again.

Did you know this is how the Bible describes our sin when Jesus forgives us? Our sins are covered and become "white as snow" (Isaiah 1:18). Jesus takes our sins' ugliness and dirtiness and covers them. So God doesn't see us in the same way we view the snowless scene—bare, dirty, and dead. He sees us as the bright, snow-covered winter landscape!

Pure.

Jesus makes us pure. But He also wants us to continue to grow and change, focusing on pleasing God in all we do. A pure heart is one that has been cleansed by Jesus. And it is a heart that wants to please God. To make Him happy.

"Blessed are the pure in heart, for they will see God," Jesus says in Matthew 5:8. When we want to grow in having a pure heart, we are careful about what we watch. We guard our eyes and ears. We are careful with our words. We think about good things—true, right, and noble things.

A pure heart is a clean heart that wants to please God. But don't forget that even when we do sin, Jesus still loves us. He still sees us and treats us as a son or daughter. He doesn't hold our sins against us. Or look down on us. So we should not try to be pure to get God to love us. He already does love us—no matter what. We should want to be pure because we love God more than anything else!

Action Step

Discuss where you need help most right now in being pure.

Prayer

Father, thank You for making us clean. You have forgiven us through Your Son, Jesus. We have been made pure. Now help us to grow in purity, always wanting to please You in what we do. In Jesus' name, amen.

55

Showing Honor

Key Verse

Do nothing out of selfish ambition or vain conceit. Rather, in humility value others above yourselves.

Philippians 2:3

Key Idea

Respect is showing honor (value) to others by our attitude and actions.

Do you have something that is valuable? What is it, and why is it important?

You might have a sports card or video game that is worth a lot. Maybe you have a special pair of shoes or an expensive piece of jewelry. It could be a toy, clothing, or a gift you received from a grandparent. Whatever it is, you probably treat it very carefully!

As amazing as those things are, do you know what is even more important in God's eyes? People!

You probably remember what the Bible says about people at the very beginning—every person is made in God's image (Genesis 1:26–27). We are truly unique or special in all of God's creation. He made us in His image and likeness so we can be friends with Him. We can love Him, trust Him, obey Him, serve Him, and bring glory to Him in everything we do!

Because we are made in God's image and likeness, every person is valuable.

Every friend you have was created by God! Your brother or sister? Yep, made by God! Your teacher at school? Yes, created by God and special to Him. Even the stranger on the street—and every person you will ever meet— matters to God. They are special to Him. Important. Valuable.

So how should we treat other people? With great **respect**!

Respect is showing honor to others by our attitude and actions. In Philippians 2:3, we are told to "value others." We can show respect by

- Doing what others want and not just what we want to do.
- Not being pushy or arguing when we disagree.
- Using kind and gentle words.
- Showing good manners.
- Not looking down on others.
- Listening more than talking.
- Being patient.

As Jesus continues to change us and make us who He wants us to be, remember that the greatest command is to love God and others. We love others when we respect them. No matter who the person is, they were made in God's image and likeness. They are valuable and deserve our respect!

Action Step

What is one way you can show respect to someone in your life?

Prayer

Father, we love You and praise You for who You are. Help us to see people the way You do. Give us a deeper love for one another. Show us how we can continue to grow in treating others with respect. In Jesus' name, amen.

56

Do You Know the Difference?

Key Verses

And this is my prayer: that your love may abound more and more in knowledge and depth of insight, so that you may be able to discern what is best and may be pure and blameless for the day of Christ.

Philippians 1:9–10

Key Idea

**Godly discernment is knowing the
difference between good and bad.**

What's the difference between a good movie and one that is, well, kind of boring? How about the difference between your favorite song and one you want to skip?

It is easy to tell the difference between our favorite food and something that tastes bad. We know the difference between a fun toy and one that gets old quickly. And it is easy to choose between our favorite hobby versus doing chores. Those are obvious and easy choices!

But knowing what is good and bad, what comes from God and what doesn't, isn't always as easy. We need discernment—godly discernment. So what is that?

The word *discern* means to separate. It is the ability to tell the difference between things.

In the Bible, discernment is more than this, though. It is way more important, and it is a character quality we can grow in with God's help.

Discernment is knowing the difference between good and bad. It is the God-given ability to see what is happening around us or inside us. Discernment helps us say no to dangerous or sinful things. Discernment helps us say yes to good, holy, and pleasing things. Without discernment, we would get ourselves in trouble a lot!

We need discernment to

. . . choose the right kind of friends.

. . . decide which movies or shows we'll watch.

. . . figure out if a song's lyrics are right and true.

. . . use words that are pure and encouraging.

. . . know what kind of people to be careful of.

. . . guard our hearts and let in only what is pure and honoring to God.

God gives us discernment as we spend time reading His Word and talking (as well as listening) to Him in prayer. We can grow in our discernment by talking to trusted family members or friends. And becoming a person who is discerning means we slow down, take our time making a decision, and think through our choices.

Action Step

Share one way you can grow in becoming more discerning.

Prayer

Father, give us wisdom. Teach us Your ways and speak to us through Your Spirit. Help us to pay attention to Your voice and do what honors You. Protect us in all that we think and do and say. In Jesus' name, amen.

57

Can You Be Trusted?

Key Verse

Go to the ant, O sluggard; consider its ways and be wise.

Proverbs 6:6

Key Idea

Being responsible means being a person others can count on.

When was the last time someone told you to be like an ant? Not like your Aunt Jennifer or Aunt Tina. We're talking about those little creatures with six legs that crawl along the ground!

It might surprise you, but the Bible tells us we can learn something from ants. Black ants. Brown ants. Big ants. Small ants. It doesn't really matter—they all kind of do the same thing and teach the same lesson.

In Proverbs 6:6, we are told to "go to the ant" and "consider its ways." The writer of Proverbs is talking to the "sluggard," or the person who is not very responsible and doesn't work hard. So Proverbs 6:6 tells us we can learn a lot from ants. If you want to be wise and not foolish, be like an ant!

You don't see ants rolling around in the mud when they should be working. You never hear ants complaining or whining. Ants don't cut corners to get the job done. In the Bible, ants are good examples of what it looks like to work hard and be responsible!

What does the Bible say about responsibility?

We are supposed to be responsible for helping others who are in need (Luke 10:30–37). To be responsible for how we use money (Proverbs 3:9–10). And responsible for caring for one another as a family (1 Timothy 5:8). Being responsible is really about being a person who can be depended on or counted on to do the right thing.

We show responsibility when we keep our word. And do our chores. When we finish our homework the right way, paying attention to all the details and working hard! If we do something wrong, being responsible means confessing it and, if we can, correcting it. Being responsible means always doing the best job you can!

So who does God want you to become? Well, in some ways, He wants you to be like an ant! Are you growing in responsibility? In what ways do others count on you?

Action Step

Write out one way you can be more responsible, starting tomorrow.

Prayer

Father, continue to teach us Your ways. Empower us to be people who work hard and do the right thing. We want to be responsible because we know it honors You and it is a way to love and serve others. In Jesus' name, amen.

58

Jesus Is Enough

Key Verses

I have learned to be content whatever the circumstances. I know what it is to be in need, and I know what it is to have plenty. I have learned the secret of being content in any and every situation, whether well fed or hungry, whether living in plenty or in want.

Philippians 4:11–12

Key Idea

Contentment is being thankful for what we *do* have instead of focusing on what we *don't* have.

"More, more, more!" Have you ever felt like all you want is more?

More toys.
More clothes.
More video games.
Just more stuff!

Our hearts can shout at us, "More, more, more!" And when they do, we need to remember something very important: Our hearts will never be satisfied with just more stuff, but only with more of Jesus!

It's not wrong to get something new. Or different. But what our hearts need most is a relationship with Jesus. He is the One who changes our hearts from saying, "I need more," to saying, "I have enough." He satisfies us, or makes us content.

We can buy a new toy or game, go on a different vacation, or move to a new city that's fun and exciting. But all those things get old after a while. We can become discontented—or sad about what we don't have. We start to think and dream about something we want.

When we are growing as followers of Jesus, He is changing us into someone who is **content**. Contentment is being thankful for what we *do* have instead of focusing on what we *don't* have.

A content person is not upset when someone else gets something.

A content person is generous with what they have.

A content person is grateful for everything they have because they know it is a gift from God.

A content person doesn't always have to buy something or go somewhere to be happy.

The Bible tells us that the Apostle Paul had "learned to be content" (Philippians 4:11). He had learned to live with whatever he had, no matter what that was. He wrote to a group of Christians saying, "I have learned the secret of being content in any and every situation, whether well fed or hungry, whether living in plenty or in want" (Philippians 4:12).

What's the secret? Jesus! We don't always need "more, more, more" because Jesus is enough for us!

Action Step

Share one way you can focus on what you do have instead of what you don't have.

Prayer

Father, our hearts need You. Help us resist the desire for just more stuff. What we need most is to know and love and serve You. Give us hearts that are thankful and see everything as a gift from You. In Jesus' name, amen.

When we are growing as followers of Jesus, He is changing us into someone who is content. Contentment is being thankful for what we *do* have instead of focusing on what we *don't* have.

Obey

Key Verse

If you love me, keep my commands.

John 14:15

Key Idea

Obedience is doing the right thing that has been asked of us with the right heart attitude.

Have you ever had to take a dog for a walk? Sometimes walking a dog can be like a game of tug-of-war! You pull the leash in one direction, and your dog pulls in the other direction. You want one thing, and your favorite pet wants another!

Learning from Jesus and learning to be like Jesus can be like that. Because we all still struggle with sin, obeying God and obeying others can be hard. Sometimes we want to do something or say something that isn't right. We may want our own way. And even when we listen and obey, we may have a bad attitude the whole time we do it.

You can make a dog obey by pulling on the leash, raising your voice to sound as serious as you can, and of course, giving them treats!

But the kind of obedience that God wants from us is different. It's deeper. He doesn't want us to pout and complain and drag our feet to obey Him or listen to others. He wants us to obey because we want to, not because we have to. Jesus wants us to obey from the heart (Romans 6:17)—a heart that listens because it loves God and loves others.

This is what Jesus meant in John 14:15 when He said, "If you love me, keep my commands." Jesus is teaching us to show our love for Him and for others when we listen and obey. The Holy Spirit is softening our hearts as we grow and change. He is helping us focus less on ourselves and more on others. Instead of obeying because we have to, we obey because we want to!

How do you act when someone asks you to do something? What about if someone asks you to do something you don't want to do—like clean your room, wash the dishes, or take out the garbage? Do you listen and obey because you love God and love others? Or just because you have to?

Action Step

What is one area at home or school where you can commit to being more obedient?

Prayer

Father, we love You and want to grow in listening more to You. Give us soft hearts so that we want to honor You and serve others by being obedient. Give us the same attitude as Christ Jesus, who obeyed You in all that He did. In Jesus' name, amen.

Taking the First Step

Key Verse

If anyone forces you to go one mile, go with them two miles.

Matthew 5:41

Key Idea

**Taking initiative means seeing something that needs
to be done and doing it before being asked.**

The trash can was overflowing. All sorts of garbage was beginning to spill over the sides onto our kitchen floor. There were paper towels, a few food scraps from dinner, and a crusty straw with strawberry milkshake stuck to the sides. It looked like a crumbling tower!

Have you ever seen a trash can like that needed to be emptied or something else that needed to be done?

Maybe you've seen a mountain of clean laundry that needed to be folded.

Dishes that needed to be put away.

A dog or cat that needed to be fed.

Someone who needed money or help with homework.

Whatever the need is, do you wait to be asked, or do you take the **initiative**? That might be a new word for you, but taking initiative just means seeing something that needs to be done and doing it without being asked.

Jesus told a story one time about going beyond what is asked. He was talking about how we can love others—even our enemies! And guess what He said? He said that the heart of His follower, or disciple, is motivated by love. A good heart is one that not only does what is asked but also meets needs without being asked.

In Matthew 5:41, He says that if someone asks us or even "forces" us to walk with them for a mile—not just down the street or around the corner, no, He says a whole mile—we shouldn't stop there.

He says we should go with them "two miles." Jesus is showing us how to love others as we should. Even when someone doesn't ask you to do something, bless them and serve them by doing it anyway. A heart that is growing in love will take the initiative to love and serve others—even without being asked!

Action Step

Share one way you can grow in taking initiative.

Prayer

Father, give us the heart of Jesus. Make us love like Him. And help us to see needs. But even more important, help us to meet those needs, even when we are not asked. In Jesus' name, amen.

Section Three

What Do I Want My Child to DO?

How should we live if Jesus is the center of our life? In this final section, we'll look at thirty ways to live differently for Jesus! Section three is all about living a more outward life, loving God, and loving others as we should.

A Life of Worship

61

Key Verse

Jesus answered, "It is written: 'Worship the Lord your God and serve him only.'"

Luke 4:8

Key Idea

**Worship is about loving God and living
for God above all other things.**

Remember that sneaky and slithering snake we met at the very beginning of the Bible? The devil has never liked when people love or live for God.

Adam and Eve, the first human beings, were made to know, worship, and serve God. They weren't meant to be at the center of the universe—God was! Only God was meant to be worshiped because of who He is.

So from the start of the Bible and the beginning of time, the devil has been trying to get people's eyes off God. He doesn't want them to love God. The devil doesn't want people serving God. Singing songs about Him. Praying to Him. Or doing anything that would show others how amazing God really is!

Satan wants to distract us and discourage us. He even tried to do this to Jesus, as we read in the New Testament.

The devil basically said that if Jesus worshiped him, he would make Jesus happy and give Him whatever He wanted (Luke 4:5–7).

He told the same old lie he told from the very beginning—from the garden when he first tempted Adam and Eve. He was trying to stop Jesus. He knew Jesus loved God the Father and came to do His will by dying on the cross for our sins. He knew Jesus was a worshiper, living for God alone!

But unlike Adam and Eve, Jesus didn't sin. He didn't fall for the devil's tricks. He didn't give in. He knew that only God deserves to be worshiped. Only God deserves our hearts and our lives.

Jesus said, "Worship the Lord your God and serve him only" (Luke 4:8).

The devil still tries to keep us from worshiping God. He'll use whatever he can to keep our hearts from growing bigger and bigger with love for God.

Living a life of worship is about giving our entire heart to God and God alone. It's about keeping Him number one—at the center. We can worship God with our time, our songs, our prayers, our money—and with our entire lives (Romans 12:1)!

Worship is about loving God and living for God above all other things.

Action Step

Share one way you can worship God no matter where you are.

Prayer

Father, guard our hearts against anything that doesn't come from You. We want to love You and live for You alone. In all that we do, help us to live a life of worship. In Jesus' name, amen.

62

Words That Heal, Not Hurt

Key Verse

The tongue has the power of life and death.

Proverbs 18:21

Key Idea

Our words have the power to heal or to hurt.

"And God said . . ."

This is one of the first things we learn about God—that He speaks. He is a powerful, loving, and ever-present God. But He is also a God who uses words. And guess what happens when He uses His words?

Light explodes out of the darkness.

Life begins to bloom and unfold.

Beauty begins to creep and crawl and cover everything!

There is power in God's words.

Because we are made in God's image, we speak too. We use words every single day. Lots of words. And like God's words, our words have power.

We might not be able to speak and then watch rain fall from the sky. Our words don't make stars dance across a thick dark summer night or make birds float from tree to tree.

But our words do have power. They have the power of "life and death" (Proverbs 18:21).

We use words to tell a friend or teacher what we want. We use words to sing along to a favorite song. Maybe we use words when we are crying. Or to tell a parent how delicious lunch or dinner was.

There's more though.

What the Bible means when it says our words have the power of "life and death" is that we can really hurt others with our words or heal others with our words. How and what we speak matters. This is why in the New Testament we are told to be careful with how we use our words. We should be "slow to speak" (James 1:19). And we are not supposed to let any "unwholesome talk" come flying off our lips, but instead we are supposed to use only words that are "helpful for building others up according to their needs, that it may benefit those who listen" (Ephesians 4:29).

So what should we do with our words? Use them as God tells us to. When we speak, God wants us to bring life, light, and encouragement to others! He wants us to use our words to heal and not hurt.

Action Step

What is one way you can use your words to build others up?

Prayer

Father, help us to talk like You talk. Fill our lips with words that bring life—words that heal and help and strengthen. Guard our lips from saying anything that might hurt others. In Jesus' name, amen.

63

Too Good to Keep to Yourself

Key Verse

My only aim is to finish the race and complete the task the Lord Jesus has given me—the task of testifying to the good news of God's grace.

Acts 20:24

Key Idea

The good news about Jesus is too good to keep to ourselves.

We love to talk about our favorite food. We share about a movie we have seen lately. We are quick to tell a friend or family member about a new toy or some kind of clothing we really like.

Talking comes easily when we are speaking about something we love!

Did you know that the first Christians told others about Jesus almost everywhere they went? They'd tell their friends. Neighbors. Even when it was hard and dangerous, they spoke up in the synagogue about how Jesus was the promised Messiah, or Savior. Some people, missionaries, even went to different towns and countries to get the word out about Jesus.

Living for Jesus is about loving Jesus. It's about learning from Him and learning to be like Him. And when we grow in our faith, we'll begin to tell others about Jesus. You don't have to go door-to-door or stand on a street corner and preach. You don't have to move to a different town or go to a different country.

Jesus wants all of us to live out our faith in front of others, and for you, maybe this means telling someone what God has been teaching you. Or sharing something you are working on changing in your life. It might be inviting a friend to your church, an event, or a concert. And maybe it is explaining to someone how to become a Christian. However you reach out, don't worry about what others think. Please God first.

And whatever you do, with your words and your actions, let others know how much you love Jesus. And how much He loves you!

Action Step

Share the name of one person you want to invite to your church.

Prayer

Father, open our eyes to those around us who don't know You. Give us the courage to talk about who Jesus is and what He has done. And give us opportunities to share this good news. In Jesus' name, amen.

64

God Is at Work through YOU

Key Verses

There are different kinds of gifts, but the same Spirit distributes them. There are different kinds of service, but the same Lord. There are different kinds of working, but in all of them and in everyone it is the same God at work.

1 Corinthians 12:4–6

Key Idea

God has gifted you to work through you.

Did you know that God wants to work through you? He doesn't want us to just learn about Him; He wants us to live for Him. And one of the main ways He works through us is by giving each of us different gifts.

That's right. There are gifts or abilities you have that are unique or special to you!

A gift is not something we earn. We don't work for it. A gift is freely given to us. This is what the Bible teaches about the gifts we have. When we become a Christian, the Holy Spirit gives us a gift—and usually more than just one!

When the Apostle Paul was writing to a church about how God wanted to work through them, he said, "There are different kinds of gifts, but the same Spirit distributes them. There are different kinds of service, but the same

Lord. There are different kinds of working, but in all of them and in everyone it is the same God at work" (1 Corinthians 12:4–6).

Gifts to help us be a leader.

Gifts to enable us to teach and explain God's truth.

Gifts to lead others to put their faith in Jesus.

Gifts that give us a soft heart toward others who are hurting.

And the list goes on!

The Holy Spirit gives each of us different gifts, but it is the same God at work in us and through us.

As you follow Jesus and serve others, He will make it clear what your gifts are. You might pay attention to what others say you are good at. Or notice where and when you get excited about doing something for God or for someone else. You can pray and ask God to help you see the ways He has gifted you.

We are all working together for Jesus—and God has gifted you in order to work through you!

Action Step

Describe one way you think the Holy Spirit has gifted you.

Prayer

Father, we don't want to live just for ourselves. We want to live for You. Show us the gifts You have given us and help us to use our gifts to love and serve others. In Jesus' name, amen.

65

True Greatness

Key Verses

Whoever wants to be a leader among you must be your servant, and whoever wants to be first among you must be the slave of everyone else. For even the Son of Man came not to be served but to serve others and to give his life as a ransom for many.

Mark 10:43–45 NLT

Key Idea

True greatness is not being served; it is serving others.

When you think of someone who is great, who do you think of and why?

Many people might think of someone famous. Or someone who is rich. A great person, some think, is someone who is in charge of others. Maybe someone who everybody notices and pays attention to.

A well-known actor or actress.

The president.

A popular singer or athlete.

An author.

Teacher.

Coach.

These are all good examples of people doing different things—many of them really great! But what is *true greatness*?

Even Jesus' first disciples struggled to understand true greatness. They, too, thought greatness was about sitting on thrones and leading others with power (Mark 10:35–37). They didn't understand Jesus' way of living. His kingdom was very different.

So He had to teach them how to live with God in charge of their lives. True greatness isn't about us. It's not about trying to look good or important in the eyes of others. It's not about others serving us and giving us what we want. True greatness is about living for others! It's about being a servant.

Who was the greatest of all? Jesus! This is why He told His first disciples and tells us today: "Even the Son of Man came not to be served but to serve others and to give his life as a ransom for many" (Mark 10:45).

Jesus came to serve and to give His life away to others, which He did by dying on the cross for our sins. How can we follow Jesus' example and be a servant to those around us?

Action Step

Share one way you can focus more on serving others rather than on being served.

Prayer

Father, give us a heart that is like Jesus'. We need Your power to live as servants—giving our lives away to others. Remind us often of what true greatness really is. In Jesus' name, amen.

Living with Open Hands

Key Verses

If anyone is poor among your fellow Israelites in any of the towns of the land the LORD your God is giving you, do not be hardhearted or tightfisted toward them. Rather, be openhanded and freely lend them whatever they need.

Deuteronomy 15:7–8

Key Idea

Living with open hands means sharing with others what God has given you.

What do you have that you could share with others?

It's not always easy to take what we have—all the things God has given us—and let others have them or use them. When the Israelites entered the Promised Land, they quickly discovered that there were people around them in need.

God instructed them to take what they had and live generously. He said don't be "tightfisted" (Deuteronomy 15:7). Instead, God told them to be "openhanded" (v. 8). In other words, don't be a person who is always saying, "Mine!" Be a person who wants to help others and share what you have with those who need it.

If the Israelites saw someone without food, they were to give them food. If someone needed clothing, they were supposed to clothe them. What about someone who needed a place to stay? The Israelites were to share their homes and let others in!

In the New Testament, Jesus warned His disciples to "watch out" for greed (Luke 12:15). A greedy person says, "How much is mine?" Or "I want more!" We are greedy when we are never satisfied and desire more and more stuff. A generous person asks, "How much can I give or share?"

Maybe this applies to your time. A favorite toy. Clothes you have or shoes sitting around in your closet. Or maybe some of your money that you could spend on more stuff, but instead you give it to someone in need.

What kind of life does Jesus want us to live? He wants us to live openhandedly. Generously. Sharing what we have with others. He wants us to love people more than we love possessions. So be willing to give even if someone doesn't give back. Work hard, and instead of spending what you earn on yourself, give it to someone in need. Freely give your time and the talents God has given you to love and serve others!

Action Step

How can you be more generous to someone in need?

Prayer

Father, You are generous with Your love toward us. Jesus poured out His life for us. He gave us what we didn't deserve. Help us love and serve others the same way You have loved us. In Jesus' name, amen.

67

Trust God

Key Verses

Trust in the Lord with all your heart
    And lean not on your own understanding;
in all your ways submit to him,
    and he will make your paths straight.

Proverbs 3:5–6

Key Idea

God knows the future, so we don't have to.

Have you ever ridden in a car when it was really foggy out?

The car lights shine just enough light to push back the dark. You can see lines on both sides of the road. The pavement in front of you stretches ahead. But the truth is, you can't see very far. Just enough road to go a little bit farther.

Or maybe you have had to wear a blindfold for a game you played. It was dark, right? And you couldn't see anything! All you could do was listen to the person's voice telling you where and how to walk.

Life can be like this sometimes. Foggy. Dark.

Maybe when you move to a new town.

Start attending a different school.

Or sometimes, something hard and scary happens to you or your family. Someone gets very sick.

When it is hard to see our way, God doesn't want us to worry. Or stress out. Remember, God is a good Father. And we are His children. No matter what we are thinking or feeling or going through, we can talk to God. He is always ready to help us and remind us of who He is.

When Peter, a disciple of Jesus, was writing to a group of Christians who were going through a tough time, he told them, "Cast all your anxiety on him because he cares for you" (1 Peter 5:7).

And Proverbs 3:5–6 says, "Trust in the LORD with all your heart and lean not on your own understanding; in all your ways submit to him, and he will make your paths straight."

When life feels a little foggy or dark, don't forget that God loves you. He has promised never to leave you (Hebrews 13:5). He will make our "paths straight." Even when we can't see the future, He can. And He is completely in control, always faithful to take care of all our needs.

Live with trust. God knows what He is doing!

Action Step

Write out Proverbs 3:5–6 to work on memorizing this week.

Prayer

Father, teach us to trust You when we don't always have the answers. Remind us that You are always in control, and that You know what is best for us. Keep us from doubting Your love. In Jesus' name, amen.

68

Loving Jesus When Life Gets Hard

Key Verse

Therefore, since Christ suffered in his body, arm yourselves also with the same attitude, because whoever suffers in the body is done with sin.

1 Peter 4:1

Key Idea

Jesus loved us in His suffering, so we should love Him in ours.

The world was once perfect. No one stubbed a toe. No one had a friend stop calling or sending text messages. Countries weren't going to war. Families weren't fighting. And there was no death. Or sickness.

There was no suffering. No bad stuff. Nothing hard.

There was *shalom*! *Shalom* simply means peace. Everything was the way it was supposed to be. But then something really bad happened.

Do you remember? Sin entered the world. Adam and Eve both said no to God. They stopped listening. They doubted He knew best. And when He told them there would be bad consequences if they rebelled against Him, they disobeyed anyway.

"And the LORD God commanded the man, 'You are free to eat from any tree in the garden; but you must not eat from the tree of the knowledge of good and evil, for when you eat from it you will certainly die'" (Genesis 2:16–17).

With sin came suffering. Hard stuff. Confusing and painful consequences. Sin hurt our relationship with God and spoiled all of God's good creation. As we have seen, God didn't leave us in our bad situation. He saved us through our faith in Jesus. Jesus suffered for us on the cross to undo what Adam and Eve had done!

But we still go through hard times, don't we?

It is tempting to think God doesn't love us when hard times hit us. Or maybe we wonder why God is letting something bad happen. We can get scared or worried. So we need to remember Jesus, to keep our eyes on Him and remember how He kept being faithful in His suffering.

Sometimes when we suffer, we don't know why. Other times we suffer because others don't like that we are living for Jesus. And sometimes, we suffer because the devil tempts us.

No matter why you suffer, keep your eyes on Jesus. Remember that He loved us in His suffering, so we should love Him in ours. He is with you and always gives you the strength to keep going!

Action Step

Name one person you can pray for who is suffering.

Prayer

Father, give us strength to love You when life is hard. Guard our hearts from doubting You or getting discouraged. And help us to keep our eyes on Jesus, who loved us by suffering for us on the cross. In Jesus' name, amen.

69

Don't Give Up

Key Verse

You need to persevere so that when you have done the will of God, you will receive what he has promised.

Hebrews 10:36

Key Idea

**Perseverance is sticking with something
or someone even when it is hard.**

The runner started the race strong. Breathing was easy. Her legs felt light, like feathers. But then, as the winding path began to turn, leading her uphill instead of downhill, everything changed.

Her legs felt heavy—like someone had strapped weights around her ankles! She worked harder and harder to catch her breath. Her chest tightened. Squinting her eyes, she still couldn't see the finish line. And then a thought popped into her mind, *Maybe I should just quit. I can't do this anymore!*

Have you ever felt that way? Maybe it wasn't running in a race or competing in a sport, but it was with your homework. Or a chore around the house that you really didn't want to do. Maybe it was when you or your family were going through a hard time.

We've probably all felt like quitting. It can feel a lot easier to just give up!

Following Jesus can be hard. *Life* can be hard. So God reminds us often in the Bible not to give up. He doesn't want us to get discouraged. He wants us to live a life of perseverance. Perseverance just means sticking with something, even when it is hard.

Stick with your friends, even when they aren't perfect.

Stick with your work.

Stick with your school.

Stick with a hobby you are learning.

And most important, stick with Jesus!

In James 1:12, we're told that those who stick with Jesus will receive a "crown of life" someday: "Blessed is the one who perseveres under trial because, having stood the test, that person will receive the crown of life that the Lord has promised to those who love him."

There is always a reward for not giving up. We can't always see what God will do or how He will honor our obedience. But He always does. Persevering is worth it!

Action Step

Share one area of your life where it can be hard to persevere.

Prayer

Father, fill us with Your Spirit. Remind us that You are at work, even when things are hard. You are growing us and changing us. Give us strength to persevere and see the reward You promise. In Jesus' name, amen.

70

WE Are the Church

Key Verses

And let us consider how we may spur one another on toward love and good deeds, not giving up meeting together, as some are in the habit of doing, but encouraging one another—and all the more as you see the Day approaching.

Hebrews 10:24–25

Key Idea

We go to church not because we *have* to but because we *want* to.

What do you think of when you hear the word **church**? Some people think of a building. Others think of a home. Some people think of a sermon, worship music, and maybe a choir.

When the Bible talks about church, it is always talking about people! And not just any people. The church is made up of people who love and follow Jesus.

In the book of Acts, the first Christians met in their homes. And we are told that when they got together as a church, they studied the Scriptures, took Communion, prayed together, and praised God. They even shared with one another if someone was in need (Acts 2:42–47).

The first Christians weren't just going to a service or program. They were a FAMILY! So they went to church not because they had to but because they wanted to. They loved each other and cared for one another. They helped one another with their gifts.

Every week, Christians still gather in different places and in different ways. So it is important for us to remember how important church is to Jesus. We can't love Jesus without loving the church—or loving one another!

Our love for Jesus helps our love for one another grow. And our love for one another helps our love for Jesus grow! This is why we need to keep going to church! Hebrews 10:24–25 says it this way: "And let us consider how we may spur one another on toward love and good deeds, not giving up meeting together, as some are in the habit of doing, but encouraging one another—and all the more as you see the Day approaching."

Some people go to church because they feel they have to go. But we should go to church because we want to! What do you love about your church?

Action Step

What is one way you can keep going to church a priority?

Prayer

Father, thank You for saving us and giving us a new family—the church. Help us remember why it is important to keep church a priority. Continue to grow our love for You, but also our love for being with one another. In Jesus' name, amen.

71

Thinking Less ABOUT Yourself

Key Verses

Do nothing out of selfish ambition or vain conceit. Rather, in humility value others above yourselves, not looking to your own interests but each of you to the interests of the others.

Philippians 2:3–4

Key Idea

**Humility is not thinking less *of* yourself;
humility is thinking less *about* yourself.**

"Vroom!"

"Bum, bum, bum, bum, ***voodoo***!"

The motorcycle came rumbling down the street. Like some kind of ancient monster clearing its throat after a long night of sleep, it belched out clouds of black smoke. Then came deep and long and loud roars. Finally, a "**BOOOOM**," like someone firing a cannon. That's when the rider brought the bike to a stop at the traffic light.

People plugged their ears.

Others squinted to see what was happening.

Everyone looked and watched.

All eyes were on the motorcycle!

If you want to know what living a humble life is like, it is the opposite of driving a noisy motorcycle! Being humble isn't about getting all the attention. Or having people look at you. Notice you. Or always listen to you.

But being humble isn't thinking less of yourself either. It's not walking around, hanging your head, or pouting. Someone who is humble is not thinking, "I am not good at this," or "I am unworthy," or "Nobody likes me."

A humble person just thinks less *about* themselves. They know they are loved and cherished by God. So they are focused on others. They are thinking about serving. Helping a friend. Listening to someone in need. They are other-centered and not self-centered.

"Do nothing out of selfish ambition or vain conceit," the Apostle Paul tells a group of Christians. We're not supposed to try to get all the attention! "Rather," he writes, "in humility value others above yourselves, not looking to your own interests but each of you to the interests of the others" (Philippians 2:3–4).

Jesus wants us to be humble. He doesn't want us to live always trying to get attention or competing with others, He wants us to have a heart like His—a humble heart focused more on loving God and others!

Action Step

Share one way you can work on being humble with your friends or family.

Prayer

Father, give us the heart of Jesus. We want a heart that is humble and focused on serving others. Forgive us for the times when we want all the attention. Give us Your love. In Jesus' name, amen.

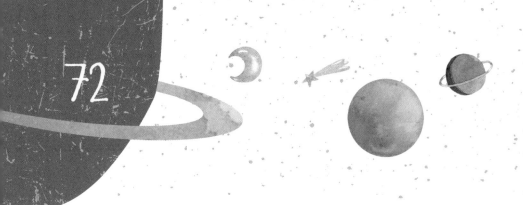

72

Be Light in the Darkness

Key Verse

Let your light shine before others, that they may see your good deeds and glorify your Father in heaven.

Matthew 5:16

Key Idea

Don't be afraid to let your light shine.

Water.
Firewood.
Graham crackers and marshmallows.
A pocketknife.
A Map. Warm clothes. Some pots and pans.
Sleeping bags. And a pillow.
These are just some of the items you might take on a camping trip! Have you ever been camping? Where did you go, and what did *you* pack?

There is one item every camper should pack. Do you know what it is? If you said, "a light," then you are right!

Whether you are sleeping in a tent or cabin or under the moon—whether hiking in the woods or through the mountains—you are going to run into DARKNESS! And what is the best way to fight the dark? With a light!

That is what Jesus said too. Not about camping, but about how we live our lives! In fact, one time when He was talking to His disciples, this is what He told them:

> You are the light of the world. A town built on a hill cannot be hidden. Neither do people light a lamp and put it under a bowl. Instead they put it on its stand, and it gives light to everyone in the house.
>
> Matthew 5:14–15

He was reminding His followers not to hide the fact that they loved God. Jesus was teaching them not to be afraid to say and do what is right. He went on to say, "let your light shine before others, that they may see your good deeds and glorify your Father in heaven" (Matthew 5:16).

Imagine spreading out your blanket on a warm summer night under the moon. The sky might look and feel dark. But can you imagine all the stars shining brightly in the darkness? Jesus is saying, "Be like that!"

Stand out.

Stand up.

Be the light everywhere you go! When we let our light shine, other people get to hear and see what God is really like.

Action Step

Share one way you or your family can be light in the darkness.

Prayer

Father, You want us to live differently. You have called us to be set apart for You. So don't let us be scared or afraid of what others think. Help us be light in the darkness. In Jesus' name, amen.

Stand out.

Stand up.

Be the light everywhere
you go! When we let our
light shine, other people
get to hear and see
what God is really like.

73

Loving by Listening

Key Verse

My dear brothers and sisters, take note of this: Everyone should be quick to listen, slow to speak and slow to become angry.

James 1:19

Key Idea

We love others by listening to others.

Close your eyes for thirty seconds and just listen. What do you hear?

Maybe you hear the sound of a refrigerator humming. Or the dishwasher swirling water. Your stomach growling. Sirens from a distance. Can you hear the wind blowing outside? What about birds chirping?

We hear noises and sounds all day—and sometimes at night. But how well do we hear one another? Do we truly love one another by the way we listen to each other?

We've already said that God speaks. He uses His words to bring about life and beauty. Things happen by the power of His words! But God doesn't just talk—He listens! He loves us by listening to us.

This is why the psalmist says, "I love the LORD, for he heard my voice; he heard my cry for mercy. Because he turned his ear to me, I will call on him as long as I live" (Psalm 116:1–2).

He hears our worries. Our fears. His ears are not closed to what concerns us and even excites us! When we sing praises to Him, He hears us. He listens to all the big stuff and the little things that are on our hearts.

Just as we are supposed to use our words to reflect God's image, we should listen to others the way He listens to us. In the New Testament, James writes to a church and reminds them of how to get along and love one another as Jesus loves us. He writes, "My dear brothers and sisters, take note of this: Everyone should be quick to listen, slow to speak and slow to become angry" (James 1:19).

He said we should be "quick to listen" and "slow to speak." When we are quick to hear someone else's needs, worries, or desires, we love like Jesus. Jesus didn't ignore people. He wasn't too busy or overly distracted. He always paid attention to others by listening to them.

How can we do the same?

Action Step

What is the biggest reason you struggle to listen to others?

Prayer

Father, thank You for loving us by listening to us. Give us Your heart for others. Teach us when to be quiet. Remind us that we love others well by listening to them more closely. In Jesus' name, amen.

74

Do Hard Things for God

Key Verse

Have I not commanded you? Be strong and courageous. Do not be afraid; do not be discouraged, for the LORD your God will be with you wherever you go.

Joshua 1:9

Key Idea

Doing holy things often means doing hard things.

What is the hardest thing someone has ever asked you to do? It could be running in a race. Completing a homework project. Or sharing your faith with a friend.

Doing hard things is, well, not easy! Anything we do that really matters or is important usually is hard. It might take time. And lots of prayer. It might mean being patient or sticking with something until it is completed. And when we don't do hard things, we miss out. Miss out on what? Well, on all that God wants to do through us.

The Bible is full of stories of men and women who did hard things for God. Really important things. Even if they seemed small at the time.

Abraham went to a country he didn't know.

Noah built an ark.

Moses led Israel through the desert.

Esther spoke to the king for her people.

Some of the prophets, like Elijah and Jeremiah, refused to stay quiet about God.

Mary said yes to God even when it didn't make sense.

And Jesus, trusting the love and wisdom of God the Father, went to the cross.

These were all hard things. They required faith and courage, and perseverance. Sometimes it meant standing out or looking foolish in the eyes of others. But they were all holy things—things done for God!

Doing something hard and holy might mean inviting a friend to church. It could be speaking out in a class or around family about your faith in Jesus. It could be doing what is right when everyone is doing wrong. It could be giving some of your money to help support others in need.

So remember, whatever you do for God will be worth the effort! Don't be afraid. "Be strong and courageous," knowing that wherever you go, "the LORD your God will be with you" (Joshua 1:9).

Action Step

Share one example of doing a hard and holy thing for God.

Prayer

Father, we belong to You. We want to be set apart, or holy. Even when You call us to do hard things, we want to be faithful. Give us faith and courage. In Jesus' name, amen.

75

The Right Feet

Key Verse

He makes my feet like the feet of a deer;
he causes me to stand on the heights.

Psalm 18:33

Key Idea

**Having the right feet is more important
than having the perfect path.**

Hiking trails can be tricky. Mountains? Even trickier!

The steep slopes and loose rocks can make walking hard. And scary. Just the smallest of slips or slides could mean a serious fall! So wearing the right kind of shoes is important.

You don't want to wear your old shoes, the ones that are bald on the bottom. And definitely not your church shoes—or fancy ones you wear to a wedding!

You want something grippy. A pair that hugs rocks, with a tread that keeps you on your feet and not on your back!

Did you know that the Bible talks a lot about walking with God? Adam and Eve walked with God. So did Abraham. And Noah. And when Jesus calls His first disciples, He invites them to come and walk with Him. Walking with God is one way the Bible describes being a friend of God and living in a relationship with Him.

There will be times when walking with God is easy. The path will be smooth and level. And then there will be times when it will be hard. It will feel like we are walking up a steep and dangerous mountain.

We need to have the right kind of feet. Sort of like having the right kind of shoes for hiking!

Having the right kind of feet means trusting God. Staying close to Him. Loving Him even when the way is difficult to understand. And staying faithful.

David, who would become one of the greatest kings of Israel, wrote of this relationship in Psalm 18:33. He looked up while in the desert of Judea and saw deer walking along dangerous and steep mountains. So he wrote, "He makes my feet like the feet of a deer; he causes me to stand on the heights."

God is the one who can make our feet strong and steady. He makes our feet like those of a deer. So remember, having the right kind of feet is more important than always having the perfect path!

Action Step

What does it mean for you to have the right kind of feet?

Prayer

Father, strengthen our faith. Give us feet like the feet of deer. Even when our path is hard, help us to keep walking with You. In Jesus' name, amen.

76

Cheering Others On

Key Verses

Therefore, since we are surrounded by such a great cloud of witnesses, let us throw off everything that hinders and the sin that so easily entangles. And let us run with perseverance the race marked out for us, fixing our eyes on Jesus, the pioneer and perfecter of faith.

Hebrews 12:1–2

Key Idea

**Cheering others on means we focus on
their success instead of our own.**

Are there people who cheer you on? Who are they, and how do they encourage you?

Imagine being in a stadium full of a large crowd. You step out on the court or field and hear the chorus of thousands of fans chanting your name. You hear and feel the roar. The excitement and enthusiasm are like a great big tidal wave carrying you into action!

If you have ever been around someone who is encouraging, that is how it can feel. Your heart swells with love and hope. Their encouragement is like the wind that blows a sailboat forward, powering it through choppy waters and waves at sea.

And we have probably all been around people who don't cheer us on. We might feel like nothing we do is right. Or ever good enough. Sometimes people see the good things we do and accomplish, and they don't say anything. Maybe they are secretly jealous. It bothers them when others succeed at a sport or hobby or in school.

We all have this same choice: Will we celebrate with others or stay silent?

In Hebrews 12:1–2, we're told that all of heaven is cheering us on. Kind of like that stadium full of people watching us perform: "Therefore, since we are surrounded by such a great cloud of witnesses, let us throw off everything that hinders and the sin that so easily entangles. And let us run with perseverance the race marked out for us, fixing our eyes on Jesus, the pioneer and perfecter of faith."

We are "surrounded" not by a few people, but by a "great cloud of witnesses." Those who have followed Jesus before us are cheering us on to do the same. They are encouraging us to keep being faithful. They are celebrating with us in our victories. And always reminding us by their example to keep "fixing our eyes on Jesus."

So as we live for Jesus, what kind of disciple does He want us to be? Someone who cheers others on!

Action Step

Share one way you can encourage someone tomorrow either with your words or a handwritten note.

Prayer

Father, thank You that we are not alone. Many who have walked with You before us are cheering us on. Help us each to be that kind of person for those around us. In Jesus' name, amen.

77

A Heart for Others

Key Verse

When Jesus landed and saw a large crowd, he had compassion on them, because they were like sheep without a shepherd.

Mark 6:34

Key Idea

Living with compassion is seeing people's needs and acting to help them.

Imagine having to walk through an entire day blindfolded. Of course, it would be dark, maybe a little dangerous. And think about everything you would miss seeing!

You wouldn't be able to see a beautiful sunrise. Outside your window, all the trees and birds would be hidden from view. But not being able to see clearly the people you love would be most painful!

One of the things that is so amazing about Jesus and how He lived is that He saw people. He noticed others and paid attention to them more than to himself. He lived without a blindfold! He wasn't indifferent to those around Him—especially those who were in need. The hurting. The sick. The blind. Those who needed a shepherd or someone to guide, protect, and take care of them.

This is what it means to live with compassion. Living with **compassion** is seeing people's needs and acting to help them. It is not just feeling sorry for someone. Or seeing someone and then not doing anything to help. True compassion is feeling someone's pain and sorrow—then doing something to help them.

It might mean listening to someone.

Praying for a friend or family member.

Helping a person in need by giving a possession or money.

Taking time to do something for someone else.

This is how Jesus loved others.

For example, in Mark 6:34, we read, "When Jesus landed and saw a large crowd, he had compassion on them because they were like sheep without a shepherd." Matthew 20:34 says, "Jesus had compassion on them and touched their eyes. Immediately they received their sight and followed him."

As God is changing us from the inside out, He is giving us a deeper love for others. He is growing us into people with a big heart and clear eyes. He is helping us take off the blindfold, to not just see people in need but to do something to help them!

Action Step

Why is it easy to live blindfolded and not notice others in need?

Prayer

Father, help us to see others the way You do. Change our hearts and help us see those who are in need. And most important, show us how we can love others in action. In Jesus' name, amen.

78

Fighting Sin

Key Verse

We are those who have died to sin; how can we live in it any longer?

Romans 6:2

Key Idea

The power of sin has been broken by Jesus, our Savior.

Like a dog being led around on a leash. Or a sled being dragged through bitter snow and cold. Like a water-skier pulled through the choppy waves behind a motorboat. Or the servant who must answer the call of a cruel master.

That is what the power of sin is like!

It can control us. Lead us. Have power over us. We think, say, and do things we know are wrong. Things that hurt others and, worst of all, things that hurt God.

That is what has been happening ever since Adam and Eve first said no to God and yes to sin. Sin has been in charge of people's hearts.

But that is sin's power before we accept Jesus as our Savior. Sin kind of runs the show! After we accept Jesus as our Savior, everything begins to change! God the Father sent Jesus the Son to die for us. He paid the penalty for our sins. He took our place on the cross. And even though we may still struggle with sin, He has demolished the power of sin.

We don't have to sin, but we sometimes choose to sin. God has sent us a Helper—the Holy Spirit. He gives us the power and strength to fight against sin and win.

The Apostle Paul says in Romans 6:2, "We are those who have died to sin; how can we live in it any longer?"

As followers of Jesus, we are called to fight sin, and not live in it. We have "died to sin." God gives us help so we can live a different kind of life. A new life. A better life. A life that looks more and more like Jesus' life.

Do you remember the fruit of the Spirit? (Galatians 5:22–23). The Bible says that as we fight sin and let the Holy Spirit control us, our lives will look different! We'll be free to love God and to love others as we should.

Action Step

Share one sin that you know you need help putting to death.

Prayer

Father, we love You more than anything. You first loved us, so help us to love You back. Give us strength and wisdom to fight sin. We want our lives to be different, so others see You in us. In Jesus' name, amen.

79

Standing Strong in the Battle

Key Verse

Put on the full armor of God, so that you can take your stand against the devil's schemes.

Ephesians 6:11

Key Idea

Be wise in the battle, not fearful.

Following Jesus is a battle. A fight.

From the very beginning, Satan has wanted to win. Remember the story of Adam and Eve? Satan wanted Adam and Eve to doubt God. Not just to doubt that God is real but to doubt that He is good and can be trusted. Satan was trying to trick them and tempt them to live for themselves.

Satan also loves to discourage us. He wants us to quit. To give up. This is what he tried to do to Jesus in the desert (Matthew 4:1–11). But Jesus didn't give in or give up. He kept saying no to Satan and remained faithful to God the Father. He saw through every lie of Satan. Filled with God's Spirit and God's Word, He beat Satan.

And of course, Satan wants to destroy any good thing God is doing in our lives or in the world. He tries to accuse us, reminding us of things we have done wrong. As hard as he has tried and still does, Satan has been defeated on the cross (Colossians 2:15).

We have been forgiven.

We don't have to fear.

Jesus rose again, conquering sin, Satan, and death.

But until Jesus comes again and defeats Satan for the final time, we are in a battle.

This is why the Apostle Paul, in Ephesians 6:11, says we should dress for battle. He says, "Put on the full armor of God." He's not talking about a metal helmet, sharp sword, or leather boots. He is talking about spiritual armor. He wants us to fill our minds and heart with God's Word and His truth and promises. He wants us to remember the good news of God's love and forgiveness. He wants us to be filled with God's Spirit, ready for battle not with our strength but with God's!

When we do, Paul says, we can stand strong "against the devil's schemes," Satan's plans against us. And so, as we follow Jesus, we shouldn't be fearful, but we should live wisely!

Action Step

Read Ephesians 6:13–18. As you read, imagine putting on each piece of God's armor.

Prayer

Father, protect us and help us to see the different ways Satan still tempts us today. Fill us with Your Spirit and teach us to be wise as we live for You. In Jesus' name, amen.

80

Little Things Are Big Things

Key Verse

Each of you should use whatever gift you have received to serve others, as faithful stewards of God's grace in its various forms.

1 Peter 4:10

Key Idea

Little things done *for* God are big things *to* God.

Has someone ever given you a gift? What was it, and who gave it to you?

We don't earn gifts. Or work to get a gift. Gifts are freely given to us by someone else. Maybe you have been given a birthday gift or Christmas present that you really wanted. Or maybe it was a gift you weren't expecting. No matter what the present was, gifts are a lot of fun to receive, aren't they?

The Bible describes how God has given each of us different gifts. We don't do anything to deserve these gifts. And even more important, the gifts God gives us are not meant just for us!

In 1 Peter 4:10, God tells us that each of us has different gifts. We've been given different abilities to be used by God and for God. We are to use "whatever gifts" we have to "serve others." Why? Because this is how God shows His love to others!

We don't have to be famous. Or have a lot of followers. We don't have to preach a sermon or go on a mission trip. We don't have to be on TV or in the movies. Jesus can use what we think are little things to do big things.

He can use your smile or kind words to encourage a friend who is feeling sad. Or He can use a selfless act, such as doing the dishes or laundry without being asked. Maybe baking cookies and taking them to a neighbor. Jesus can work through you when you invite a friend to church or youth group. He can use a poem you write, a card you make, or a song you sing. These examples might seem like little things, but when we do them out of our love for God and others, they are big things to God!

So, what gift has God given you? Who does Jesus want you to serve this week? How can you show His love in simple and practical ways? Because don't forget, the gifts we have been given are not just for us—God wants to pour out His love in you and through you!

Action Step

Choose one simple way to serve a friend or family member this week.

Prayer

Father, help us to think more about others than ourselves. Give us opportunities to show our love in small ways. Remind us that little things can be big when we do them out of love for You and others. In Jesus' name, amen.

81

Welcoming Others

Key Verse

Abraham looked up and saw three men standing nearby. When he saw them, he hurried from the entrance of his tent to meet them and bowed low to the ground.

Genesis 18:2

Key Idea

Living with a welcoming heart is living with an open heart for others.

Have you ever felt like an outsider? Maybe you were new at school. Or you were going to youth group or a Sunday School class for the first time. It can be uncomfortable when you feel like a stranger!

All of us probably have been in a situation where we were new or when there were new people around us. So how do you respond when you see someone no one is talking to? What do you do when you notice a classmate or teammate by themselves? What about when you see someone sitting alone?

In the Old Testament, Abraham is a good example of someone who welcomed others. Or we might say someone who showed hospitality. In Genesis 18, there is a story about how he was sitting by some trees near the entrance of his tent. It was hot. Dusty. He was probably tired. And then something happened.

Abraham looked up and saw three men standing nearby. They were new. Outsiders. These men weren't friends or family members. Guess what Abraham does. He hurries or runs to welcome them!

He doesn't act like he doesn't see them.

He doesn't ignore them.

He doesn't think, *Hmmm, I'm sure someone else will talk to them.*

No, he runs. And then he brings them into his tent, where he and his wife, Sarah, serve them and bless them by cooking them a delicious meal. That is pretty welcoming!

Did you know God wants to use you to bless others? He wants to work through you to show His love to others. And just as God has welcomed us, He wants us to welcome others. Living with a welcoming heart is living with an open heart for others. How can you show God's love to others by welcoming them?

Action Step

Share one reason it can be hard to welcome others.

Prayer

Father, You have accepted us. We belong to You. Help us to treat others the way You have treated us. Give us an open and welcoming heart. And teach us to see people who need a place to belong and feel accepted. In Jesus' name, amen.

82

Choosing the Right Kind of Friends

Key Verse

Do not be misled: "Bad company corrupts good character."

1 Corinthians 15:33

Key Idea

Your friends will either make you more like Jesus or less like Jesus.

Who are your closest friends, and why?

We were created for relationships. All of us need friends. We weren't meant to go through life alone. But we aren't meant to have just any kind of friends—we must choose the right kind of friends!

In 1 Corinthians 15:33, we are reminded that "bad company corrupts good character." And in the Old Testament, we are told that we need to "walk with the wise" because when we do, we "become wise, for a companion of fools suffers harm" (Proverbs 13:20).

Have you ever noticed how you start to act like those you are spending time with? Maybe you notice it in how you dress. Or the movies you watch and the music you listen to. The things you care about or don't care about. We can see changes in our attitudes, words, or actions toward others.

This is why we are reminded to be careful of foolish friends. They will form us or shape us. So we are not to be "misled." As followers of Jesus, we need friends who are following Jesus too.

We need friends who love God, who will make us want to become better, not worse. We need friends who are honest and trustworthy. Friends who care about doing what is right and honoring God—not friends who talk about others or about us when we aren't around. We need friends we can count on. The kind of people who will be there for us no matter what, who cheer us on and want what is best.

We also need to be the right kind of friend to others. But we need to choose our friends wisely. And sometimes that means choosing different friends. Or not spending as much time with some friends. Guard your heart. Guard your love for Jesus. Guard who you choose to be friends with. Your friends will either make you more like Jesus or less like Jesus!

Action Step

What is one way you can be more careful about who you spend time with?

Prayer

Father, You have made us to be in relationship with others. Help us to see why choosing the right kind of friends is so important. Protect us from foolish friends and give us the relationships that will make us more like Jesus. In Jesus' name, amen.

83

Don't Be Afraid to Dream

Key Verse

I can do all this through him who gives me strength.

Philippians 4:13

Key Idea

We are all called to follow Jesus, but we each follow Jesus differently.

God created you special. Unique. The gifts and abilities He has given you are not by accident! You are who you are because God made you that way.

Sometimes it is easy to look at someone else and see what they are good at. Or we notice different gifts or abilities we wish we had. But God has made you the way you are for a reason. And He wants you to discover that too, which can take time and sometimes the help of others.

When Jesus called His first disciples to "Come, follow me" (Matthew 4:19), He was inviting them to live for Someone bigger than themselves! Jesus calls each of us to follow Him. He wants to work in us and through us. And so, as we follow Jesus, we will also all follow Jesus differently.

The way *you* live for God might be very different from how your brother or sister or mom or dad follows Jesus.

God wants His people everywhere as light in the darkness! He wants

- Teachers
- Mechanics
- Moms and dads
- Doctors
- Carpenters
- Pastors and missionaries

Okay, you get the point!

All these examples are different from one another. But no matter what we do, the purpose is the same.

Jesus wants us to do whatever our work is for God and for others. So dream big. Ask yourself, *How does God want to use me?* Pay attention to what you love and the things that interest you or that you are good at. Ask your mom or dad or a friend to help you see how you are uniquely made.

God has wired you for a purpose. He doesn't want you to go through life just living for yourself! He has plans and purposes just for YOU.

Action Step

Describe a unique quality about yourself and how you can begin to use that for God.

Prayer

Father, You created us for a purpose. You want us to see how unique and special we are. Help us see how we can honor You and live for You as we continue to follow You. In Jesus' name, amen.

84

Positive in the Face of Problems

Key Verse

Then Caleb silenced the people before Moses and said, "We should go up and take possession of the land, for we can certainly do it."

Numbers 13:30

Key Idea

Because of who God is, we can be positive even in the face of problems.

Have you ever felt too small for a job that felt too big?

That's how God's people, the Israelites felt when they were getting ready to go into the land God had promised Abraham, Isaac, and Jacob. Sometimes the Bible calls this land Canaan. Today, it is most often called Israel.

Moses had been instructed to send some men—spies—to go and check out the land. They were to explore the people and places to see what God's people were up against. And boy, they did *not* like what they saw!

The people living in the land looked like giants. Or monsters. They were huge. So big that it made the Israelites feel like "grasshoppers" (Numbers 13:33). The cities were massive. They were well built and protected with thick and tall walls. When these spies returned to give a report to Moses and the Israelites, they were terrified. And they made everyone else scared too!

Except for one man. One spy. One follower of God. His name was Caleb.

He saw things differently. Caleb didn't start to pout or cry or get a bad attitude. There was no complaining or being negative. And he wasn't scared or intimidated. He saw the same enemies of God, the same land, and the same cities. But do you know what he said?

He told all the Israelites to be quiet! He "silenced" them and then said, "We should go up and take possession of the land, for we can certainly do it" (Numbers 13:30). Did you catch that? When everyone was saying, "we can't do it," Caleb said, *"we can certainly do it!"*

Caleb knew who his God was. He knew that God could do anything. He lived with faith and courage. And he was positive, even in the face of problems! Are you someone who others want to be around? Someone who lives with a positive faith that shows in your attitude and actions?

Action Step

Share one way you can demonstrate a more positive attitude in all you do.

Prayer

Father, nothing is too hard for You. You can do all things, and we can trust You no matter what. Help us to live with faith and joy—always showing a positive attitude because we know You are in control. In Jesus' name, amen.

85

But First, Love God

Key Verse

But seek first his kingdom and his righteousness, and all these things will be given to you as well.

Matthew 6:33

Key Idea

The first or most important priority in our lives is loving God.

What is the first thing you do when you wake up? How about the first thing you do when you get to school? If you play a sport or musical instrument, is there something you do first when you are getting ready to play?

First, I need to brush my teeth.

First, I need to say hello to my friends or teacher.

First, I need to stretch.

What we do first is usually the most important thing.

Jesus talked about firsts too.

One day, when He was teaching His followers not to worry, He told them to do something FIRST!

Don't worry about your clothes, He told them, or about what you will eat or drink; their Father knew about all of that and would take care of them, he said (Matthew 6:31–32). Jesus wanted them to know God.

"Seek first his kingdom and his righteousness, and all these things will be given to you as well," Jesus taught them (Matthew 6:33). Put God at the center. Love Him above everything. No matter what you do, live each day trying to please God—FIRST! And guess what will happen? God will take care of everything else.

This is similar to what the psalmist says in the Old Testament when he was praying to God about being first. He prayed, "Teach me your way, Lord, that I may rely on your faithfulness; give me an **undivided heart**, that I may fear your name" (Psalm 86:11, emphasis added).

God doesn't want us to live with just half a heart for Him. He doesn't want to be second or third or fourth. He wants to be, and deserves to be, first. Living with an undivided heart is living with God first!

Action Step

What is one way to keep God first in your life?

Prayer

Father, You are worthy of our lives. We want You to be first. Help us to love You and serve You in everything we do. In Jesus' name, amen.

86

Speak Up and Stick Up!

Key Verses

Speak up for those who cannot speak for themselves,
for the rights of all who are destitute.
Speak up and judge fairly;
defend the rights of the poor and needy.

Proverbs 31:8–9

Key Idea

Be strong for the weak.

Has someone ever come to your rescue or defense? Maybe you were sick, and a family member helped take care of you—giving you food and medicine when you needed it most. Or maybe there was a time when you were injured, and someone provided first aid. Has anyone ever given you money when you didn't have any? What about a friend or family member who stuck up for you?

What we need most when we are weak is someone who is STRONG!

At times, we need someone to carry us. To speak words that encourage us or defend us. We need someone to protect us. And when someone does wrong to us, we need someone who will fight for us for what is right.

The Bible says this is the kind of person God wants us to be for others. In Proverbs 31:8–9, we are encouraged to walk, or live, in God's ways—with wisdom. So what does that look like? We are to "Speak up for those who cannot speak for themselves, for the rights of all who are destitute. Speak up and judge fairly; defend the rights of the poor and needy."

In the New Testament, James 1:27 tells us, "Religion that God our Father accepts as pure and faultless is this: to look after orphans and widows in their distress and to keep oneself from being polluted by the world."

As followers of Jesus, we are called to love the least among us. We aren't supposed to love only those who are like us. We are to be the kind of people who love and care for those who are in need and are hurting. God wants us to do right for those who have been wronged.

Jesus was always welcoming the outsider, the person who wasn't a part of the in crowd. He was a friend to those who didn't have friends. He cared for the person who was sick or poor or without a family. He had a special place in His heart for the brokenhearted. He was strong for everyone He met who was weak.

Action Step

Name a person or group considered weak. What is one way you can help?

Prayer

Father, You are close to the hurting and brokenhearted. Give us Your love. Help us to see who You are calling us to strengthen. Show us how we can stand up and speak up for those who are weak. In Jesus' name, amen.

87

Living with Integrity

Key Verse

Whoever walks in integrity walks securely,
but whoever takes crooked paths will be found out.

Proverbs 10:9

Key Idea

Do what is right even when no one is watching or listening.

A driver taps the brakes and slows down when they see a police officer parked along the side of the road. Someone is careful with their words when talking to a brother or sister after they realize a parent can hear them. Or maybe someone looks at something on their phone or the television when they think that what they are doing is hidden.

These are just a few examples of how hard it can be to do what is right all the time, no matter what. But God doesn't want us to love Him just when it is easy. He doesn't want us to obey Him out of fear or obligation. He wants our hearts. And with His help, we can always do what is right. After all, obeying Him is what is best for us too!

The true test of who we are is whether we do what is right even when no one is watching or listening. This is what it means to have integrity—or to live with integrity.

Proverbs 10:9 says, "Whoever walks in integrity walks securely, but whoever takes crooked paths will be found out."

There is an important word in that verse, *securely*. What God is saying is that choosing to live with integrity protects us. We live safely or securely.

A person of integrity doesn't have to work hard to hide something. A person of integrity doesn't have to fear getting caught. A person of integrity has peace and joy because they know what they are doing honors and pleases God. And that is a good feeling!

Proverbs 10:9 also gives us a warning. It says that those who "take crooked paths will be found out." Even when we think no one is watching, God is. Eventually, our choices become visible to others.

But don't forget, even when we fail or fall short, God is always ready to forgive us and give us a new start. He loves us too much to ever leave us.

Action Step

Write down and memorize Proverbs 10:9.

Prayer

Father, give us a heart that wants to obey You. Fill us with Your Spirit so we choose to do what is right all the time. Protect us as we build character and live for You in the world. In Jesus' name, amen.

88

Honoring Those in Authority

Key Verses

Children, obey your parents in the Lord, for this is right. "Honor your father and mother"—which is the first commandment with a promise— "so that it may go well with you and that you may enjoy long life on the earth."

Ephesians 6:1–3

Key Idea

Obeying those in authority is a way of loving and trusting God.

Being a parent is hard. There is a lot to do and think about and take care of! While no parent is perfect, every parent has been given a special job or role by God—they have been given to YOU as a mom or dad.

We might say that God has put them in charge, or given them authority. Authority is not a bad thing—it is meant to be good. Parents are meant to love and lead their children toward Jesus. And what are children supposed to do? Obey and honor their parents (Ephesians 6:1–3).

Obeying those in authority is not just a rule for children at home. We have people in authority over us at school (a teacher), in government (our city, state, and national leaders), the police, a sports team we play on, etc. Obeying those in authority should never include doing something wrong or allowing someone to do something that we know isn't right. But listening to those who are leading us shows our love for God and trust in Him.

And we are not only supposed to obey those in authority but also to pray for them. Why? Because it is hard work to lead others and do what is right!

First Timothy 2:1–2 says, "I urge, then, first of all, that petitions, prayers, intercession and thanksgiving be made for all people—for kings and all those in authority, that we may live peaceful and quiet lives in all godliness and holiness."

Obeying those in authority might look like listening and obeying with a joyful attitude. Being respectful with our words. Standing up and greeting someone who is older. And by always remembering that authority was God's idea, and He gives it to us for our good!

Action Step

Share one way you can show proper respect for those in authority.

Prayer

Father, remind us that obeying others is a way for us to show our love and trust in You. Following You and loving others is more important than doing whatever we want. Give us a heart that honors and respects those You have given us for our good. In Jesus' name, amen.

89

An Arrow in the Hands of God

Key Verse

Like arrows in the hands of a warrior
are children born in one's youth.

Psalm 127:4

Key Idea

In God's hands, you are an arrow of truth, goodness, and beauty.

For a game, have you ever battled against a friend or family member? Was it a pillow fight, a water fight, or Nerf gun war?

Real battles aren't fun. And they are not games! They are for real. And so are the weapons. In ancient times, soldiers would suit up in armor. Sharpen their swords. Then head into battle against an enemy.

One of the most important weapons soldiers had long ago were arrows. Arrows would zip and zing through the air to reach their targets and defeat enemies.

But did you know that the Bible calls *you* an arrow? Children are described in different ways in the Old Testament. You are a blessing. A great reward. You are of great worth and value because you are made in the image of God (Psalm 127:3–5).

Psalm 127:4 gives one of the most interesting descriptions of who *you* are. It says, "Like arrows in the hands of a warrior are children born in one's youth."

You are an arrow in the hands of God.

You are not an arrow that is supposed to harm or hurt people. You are not an arrow in the same way that arrows were used in ancient times. As a follower of Jesus, you are an arrow of life and light. You are to live as a kind of "weapon" against all of the dark, ugly, and painful stuff in our world! You are to be an arrow of truth, goodness, and beauty.

When you love the unlovable, you are an arrow.

When you forgive, you are an arrow.

When you are generous with your time or money, you are an arrow.

When you serve and bless others, you are an arrow.

Arrows in God's hands bring love, hope, and joy wherever they go. In a world that is full of so much hurt, arrows in God's hands are needed now more than ever!

Action Step

How can you live as an arrow in God's hands?

Prayer

Father, thank You for wanting to work through us to accomplish Your purposes in the world. Help us to remember how much the world needs us to live for You. Show us how we can be arrows in Your hands. In Jesus' name, amen.

90

An Out-of-the-Ordinary Life

Key Verse

Make every effort to live in peace with everyone and to be holy; without holiness no one will see the Lord.

Hebrews 12:14

Key Idea

To be holy is to live an out-of-the-ordinary life for God.

What do you think of when you hear the word *holy*? Hopefully, not something bad or boring! Or like a sickness you don't want to catch.

The Bible describes God as holy. In the Old Testament book of Isaiah, we read about how the prophet saw a vision of heaven. God was seated on His throne, and angels were worshiping and calling to one another, "Holy, holy, holy is the LORD Almighty; the whole earth is full of his glory" (Isaiah 6:3).

Three times they repeat that the Lord is holy, holy, holy.

Holy means to be set apart. God is completely and entirely set apart from anything that is evil or sinful. He is perfect in all His attributes (or who He is). And so, because God is holy and because we belong to God, we are called to be holy.

This is why we are commanded to "Make every effort to live in peace with everyone and to be holy; without holiness no one will see the Lord" in Hebrews 12:14.

Jesus died so we could be forgiven and made holy. But we also must grow in holiness. This takes time, like our entire lives! We grow and are changed by God's grace, little by little. But because we love Jesus so much, He gives us a heart that wants to be holy—that wants to live differently for Him and with Him.

To be holy is to live set apart for God. It is to live differently than others are living. It is to live an out-of-the-ordinary life. So holiness is not bad; it is good. Whatever you do, do it for God. Be holy, for God is holy!

Action Step

Share one way you will live an out-of-the-ordinary life for God.

Prayer

Father, help us to grow in holiness. Give us the power to live differently—out of the ordinary. Make our lives count for You. And shine in and through us by Your Spirit. In Jesus' name, amen.

Dr. Patrick Schwenk (DMin, Biola University Talbot School of Theology) is a pastor of nearly twenty-five years and the coauthor with his wife, Ruth, of *Faith Forward Family Devotional*, *For Better or For Kids: A Vow to Love Your Spouse with Kids in the House*, and *In a Boat in the Middle of a Lake: Trusting the God Who Meets Us in Our Storm*.

Ruth Schwenk is the founder of the popular blog TheBetterMom.com, and with Patrick founded the blog FortheFamily.org and the podcast RootlikeFaith .com. She is the trusted author of several books, including *Jesus, Calm My Heart*, *Trusting God in All the Things*, *Settle My Soul*, *Pressing Pause*, *The Better Mom Book*, and *The Better Mom Devotional*.

The Schwenks are Michigan football superfans and self-proclaimed foodies. They met while attending the Moody Bible Institute in Chicago and have been married for twenty-five years. They live with their four children, two pugs, and a loyal Labrador retriever in the beautiful area of Ann Arbor, Michigan.